Making God in OUR Image

John L. Kachelman Jr.

Published by Kachelman Publications
http://www.kachelmanpublications.com

ADDITIONAL COPIES AND MATERIALS AVAILABLE ONLINE.

ISBN: 0692680829
ISBN-13: 978-0692680827

Dedication

To those who have encouraged me to hold fast to the sound doctrine of Holy Scripture! This includes a number of congregations of God's People and a myriad of faithful beloved brethren who have supported and given me strength. When you are "kicked to the curb" by modern idolaters and cynically dismissed by the blasphemous deconstructionists, it is a God-send to have the sweet fellowship that is found among God's faithful!

Table of Contents

Foreword:
"Who Is God?"

Isaiah's response to a culture that had replaced the Almighty God with idols made in their own image was blunt, "You turn things upside down!" (Isaiah 29:16, ESV).

We live in a hostile environment where culture challenges the very foundation of our belief systems. One of the clearest illustrations of this is the way in which modern culture has attempted to redefine "God." The biblical "fear" for the Almighty Jehovah of the Holy Bible has been replaced with a watered-down Deity of "manageable" proportions viewed as a kind "grandfatherly" Sovereign who immediately grants every wish or is cherished as an omnipotent "lucky charm" able to protect us with unfailing success.

This prevailing attitude is addressed in this lesson series. The lessons take a long, hard look at how modern culture has redefined God. A more troubling observation in these lessons is the way that Believers have allowed this cultural redefinition to infect their faith, worship, and service to the Almighty God. The chaotic idolatry at the foot of Mt. Sinai is seen once again in our modern society. Let us open the Scriptures, examine the Almighty God revealed within, recognize the idolatry of redesigning God, and repent while there is yet time! This lesson series has pulled together many resource works that are cited in the notes. There is one work that helped spur this series more than any other. It was while reading *The Trivialization of God* (written by Donald W. McCullough) that this series was conceived. Consequently, I will refer to this work often to illustrate various points.

Introduction for Teachers

This material is designed to be used in a variety of educational forums. The series was originally designed as a sermon series to be presented from the pulpit. Upon request, the series materials were reformatted and expanded so they would be suitable for a class study and discussion.

Your purchase of this book also entitles you to a free digital download of the lesson series materials from Kachelman Publications (use the code below for the free download at www.kachelmanpublications.com). This digital download includes a digital version of this book, individual lessons, handouts and PowerPoint slideshows for lessons. These materials should help you present the study and provide resources for teaching the series.

This free digital download includes permission to print the files as needed for use in the Bible class but *does not allow the sale, transfer, copying, or dissemination* of any kind of the digital files from the purchaser to any other user. The purchaser of this book has permission to make copies of the handouts for the class; however this permission does not allow them to give an entire copy of the study to another person to use. An additional purchase of the digital download is required by other individuals other than the original purchaser. *Please note*: if a congregation purchases these materials, they can be used multiple times for different classes in that congregation.

In the lesson text you will find the computer mouse symbol that indicates where you should click to advance the animation and reveal the next point or slide in the presentation. These symbols should appear on Lessons 1-10 (the last two lessons were originally articles and do not have PowerPoint slides since they were not presented during the class study).

> **CODE: IMAGE2016**
> Enter this code after adding item to cart

- 1 -

Losing the Biblical Awe

(Exodus 20:18-19; 32:1-4)

Introduction

I.   🖱 We begin a series that focuses attention upon a critical topic—GOD! Our personal concept of God is the most important thing in our belief system. This is not necessarily the concept of God that we visibly demonstrate in worship and words, but it is the concept of God that we hold within our hearts that is the compass guiding our actions. The disconnection between the belief of God in the heart and its practice in daily choices is expressed by the Lord's condemnation of the idolaters in His day. These idolaters professed to believe in the Jehovah God of the Scriptures but in reality believed in another "god" to whom their devotion and worship was expressed. They professed to believe in one God but their personal concept conveyed that they actually believed in "another god." "You hypocrites, rightly did Isaiah prophesy of you: 'This people honors Me with their lips, But their heart is far away from Me. But in vain do they worship Me, Teaching as doctrines the precepts of men.'" (Matthew 15:7-9).

Those in the very presence of the Lord Jesus Christ had taken the God of the Scriptures and remade Him into their own image! The consequential judgment

1

upon their actions was severe: they were "hypocrites"; their religious devotion was shallow "lip service"; their true devotion was to an object "far from" Jehovah God; and their structure for religious devotion was "precepts of men." Their religious devotion was NOT acceptable. Although they were "sincerely" guided by their "devout feelings" and they followed "doctrine and teachings," their religion was directed to something other than the Almighty God—hence it was vain! This singular fact is a shocking realization to those who understand the damnable consequences of a "vain religious practice."

A. No person ever rises above his idea of God.

The greatest factor in religion is not what one's mouth confesses to believe (although this is important) but what one's heart believes God to be. The heart puts into action the true belief concepts (hence one is urged to be "obedient from the heart" (Romans 6:17).

There is a secret law of the soul that moves one toward the mental image of God (Romans 1:21-23). Our "God" is the product of our heart's convictions.

B. A.W. Tozer, a denominational minister with the evangelical denomination Christian and Missionary Alliance, was very concerned that contemporary Christian living set the church on a dangerous course toward compromising with "worldly" concerns. Among his writings are two books that are considered "classics": *The Pursuit of God* and *The Knowledge of the Holy*. These books stress that the Believer must pursue knowledge of the Holy God and this knowledge must never be compromised by worldliness. Here are some thoughts from his book, *The Knowledge of the Holy*:

1. *"The gravest question before the Church is always God Himself ...the most revealing thing about the Church is her idea of God ...the mightiest thought the mind can entertain is the thought of God...Our real idea of God may lie buried under the rubbish of conventional religious notions" (1-3).*

2

2. *"The man who comes to a right belief about God is relieved of 10,000 temporal problems, for he sees at once that these have to do with matters which at the most cannot concern him very long"* (4).

3. Since one's belief about God is so critical, for one to corrupt the truth about God is an inexcusable act (Psalm 50:21). *"Among the sins to which the human heart is prone, hardly any other is more hateful to God than idolatry, for idolatry is at bottom a libel on His character. The idolatrous heart assumes that God is other than He is...and substitutes for the true God one made after its likeness. Always this God will conform to the image of the one who created it and will be base or pure, cruel or kind, according to the moral state of the mind from which it emerges. A God begotten in the shadows of a fallen heart will quite naturally be no true likeness of the true God...The essence of idolatry is the entertainment of thoughts about God that are unworthy of Him. It begins in the mind...The idolater simply imagines things about God and acts as if they were true"* (5).

4. When idolatry is transferred from one member's heart into the hearts of other members in the congregation and ultimately it is transferred into the entire congregation, disaster results. *"The first step down for any church is taken when it surrenders its high opinion of God...The masses of her adherents come to believe that God is different from what He actually is; and that is heresy of the most insidious and deadly kind. The heaviest obligation lying upon the Christian Church today is to purify and elevate her concept of God until it is once more worthy of Him"* (7).

II. Have you given serious thought to the God of your beliefs?

How do you imagine God? How well do you know God? Does the angelic praise (Revelation 4:8b) or the idolatrous form (Psalm 50:21) reflect your beliefs about God? This is a disturbing query, but it must be asked.

Pharaoh's question – "Who is the Lord that I should obey His voice...?" (Exodus 5:2) -- deserves answering. How will you answer it? This series will offer you a basis for answering.

III. ⌖ Think about the way in which God is viewed today.

Visit many church worship services on Sunday morning and you will likely find a congregation comfortably relating to a deity who fits nicely within their precise doctrinal positions, who lends almighty support to their social crusades, or who is exactly what they desire in spiritual experiences. But there will be an absence of awe! Does this group dare approach the Almighty God yet feel no awe, no sweaty palms, and no shaky knees? The atmosphere is often totally different from that found in the Scriptures (Revelation 1:17; Hebrews 12:28-29).

A. ⌖ *"Reverence and awe have been replaced by a yawn of familiarity. The consuming fire has been domesticated into a candle flame"* (McCullough, 13).

B. ⌖ *"Does anyone have the foggiest idea what sort of power we so blithely invoke?"* (Dillard, 40).

C. Highlighting the thesis of this study is an insightful comment from the sixteenth century:

⌖ *"The human mind is, so to speak, a perpetual forge of idols. There was a kind of renewal of the world at the deluge, but before many years elapsed, men are forging gods at will... The human mind dares to imagine a god suited to its own capacity; it substitutes vanity and an empty phantom in the place of God... The mind, in this way, conceives the idol, and the hand gives it birth"* (Calvin, 54-55).

D. ⌖ To be honest, many have accepted a concept of the God of the Bible and whittled it down to a manageable proportion; they refashion God to fit *their* expectations and to serve *their* desires. God thus becomes the Patron of a specific political party; the Specter for one overruling cause; and the Censor for one specific belief. Consequently, modern man has exchanged the glory of the

4

incorruptible God for a god that is more convenient in his selfish perspectives. The result—biblical awe is lost.

This lost awe is sadly illustrated in Bible class notes that were used in a congregation of God's People as it discussed how to approach God in worship— all awe of the Almighty's sovereign command was diluted and any trembling respect of the Sovereign's holiness was erased.[1] Look at some of the excerpts:

1. *"We humans are capable of expressing worship toward God by a variety of emotional and physical responses"* (Notes 1:2).

2. *"Each of us will see God differently, and seek to worship Him differently. It is my belief that God has given to each of us a personality type that seeks to worship Him differently from other personality types. David could dance naked before the Ark as an act of worship. Abraham would give God ten percent of his booty; Hannah would give God her son. Mary would worship Him by pouring expensive perfume on His feet and washing it with her hair...Our God enjoys spontaneous, loving, heart-felt responses of any nature as long as they are authentic"* (Notes 1:6).

3. *"David's responses came from the heart. He did what his heart told him to do and it was acceptable to God as worship, because it was authentic!"* (Notes 1:9).

4. *"(The God of our) Worship is different from one person to the next"* (Notes 1:10).

5. *"Our God has a strange taste for He loves Rejoicing, Spontaneity, and Graciousness. He enjoys watching His children have fun and enjoy themselves...If He didn't specifically command it then it must not be as important to Him as it is to us"* (Notes 4:12-13).

6. Whenever it comes to pleasing God, the requisite is, *"We need to express joy (6:2)...God is happy with each individual's efforts to worship Him...I might not appreciate the method by which another human honors and*

5

glorifies God, but I'm not God and I cannot speak for Him. A god who could make orangutans, rhinos, coo-coo birds, pelicans, and a host of other strange and unique creatures has to be a God who can at least tolerate, if not love STRANGE THINGS!...there needs to be a spirit of love and acceptance for the variety of human expression...love means letting others be themselves, express themselves as they feel the need" (Notes 7:13).

7. *"My task is to do what I think God wants of me to be pleasing to Him and let the right be the same for the next guy"* (Notes 7:14).

8. *"Praise happens when we let each other BE OURSELVES—to worship God in our own unique and different way"* (Notes 7:14).

E. Is it possible that modern culture's "tolerance" has allowed such a philosophy to seep into your reasoning processes? Is it possible this ungodly tolerance has happened in your home congregation? It is this disturbing possibility that our series seeks to explore and answer.

Body

I. **ISRAEL—Losing the Holy Awe at Mt. Sinai!**

A. Israel was liberated from Egyptian slavery by the visible power of Almighty God. The nation marched to Sinai and there beheld the visible power of God. All of this was too much for the nation (Exodus 20:18-19). Who can blame them for their fear? Their request was just, but their awe was lost. They wanted a god that was more to their liking. They did not intend to abandon God; they just wanted a better concept of Him, one that was more meaningful to them and one that would relate to their needs (Exodus 32:1-4).

B. Israel's loss resulted from three steps.

1. She lost her awe of the Almighty.

Israel forgot that God was far different from what she could imagine. She wanted a god who would be useful to her immediate needs and would conform to her concepts. Imagining a different deity, she made this deity never thinking she had abandoned God (Exodus 32:4b).

2. 🖰 She was impatient with God's silence (Exodus 32:1).

God seemed too distant; too slow; to unaccommodating. Israel wanted something immediately; something more satisfying.

3. 🖰 She allowed individualism to rule.

"Make us" and "we do not know" are terms expressing Israelite feelings that they ought to be in complete control of the situation. Forgetting she had yielded to God's control (Exodus 20:18-19), she pressed the fact that each had the *right* to make personal demands about the kind of god he/she desired (Exodus 32:23).

II.   🖰 **The Church—Losing the Holy Awe Today!**

The history of religion reveals that there has always been the temptation to forsake God for other gods (1 Corinthians 8:5). Even in the Garden of Eden idolatry was a problem because man sought to be *like* God (Genesis 3:5). This temptation continues to present problems to modern believers.

A. We struggle with a lost awe for God.

1. Modern minds often hold a greater awe for the mysteries of scientific technology than for the Almighty God. Confidence in science encourages us to just wait for ignorance to be answered by scientific methods.

2. The scientific revolution has pushed God into the shadows of life. The unknown answers which belong to God (Deuteronomy 29:29) are crowded out by the flood of facts and measurable data. God has been forced into retirement as totally unnecessary.

Pushed out by Theory & assumption

7

3. Reliance upon Science has led many to accept psychology's conclusion that any belief in God is really a projection of one's psyche and is only the image of that person's desires. Sociology has reduced God to a mere human cultural concept.

4. Today's unanswerable questions exist only because Science has not yet brought every element of Nature under control. With more time, more money, and more research all unknowns will be answered.

5. A casualty of this reverence for science is the Believer's awe in the Almighty God. No longer do we place matters of ignorance into the Almighty's hands and find contentment. No longer are we awed at the thought of approaching the Almighty and we will not feel terror as Abram (Genesis 15:12), hide as Moses (Exodus 3:6), fall as Saul (Acts 9:4), or cry as Isaiah (Isaiah 6:5).

B. We are impatient with God's silence.

1. Many feel God's silence means He is distant from us; unconcerned about us.

2. Many want to *feel* God's nearness and state that the God of the Bible is not real enough.

3. Many face problems in life that find release through affluence. So God becomes a casualty. There is no real need for God when we are able to provide our own cures.

4. Those who face problems without available cures cry out to God but hear only silence—no reassuring voice; no strong arm to help. Only acute loneliness and excruciating emptiness of the soul. This brings about indifference. Living in a world where technological innovations have made communication instant, we want an instant answer from God. But our desperate plea to hear God's authoritative voice is met with silence. We are tempted to fashion a God that communicates and leads and speaks to us as we desire.

8

C. 🖱 We are victims of rampant individualism.

1. No other country is as prone to this as the United States of America. Freedom is our most precious national asset and modern minds have made individualism a national religion. Whatever else we believe, all will believe that "each one must believe his/her way and it is wrong to force group beliefs upon others."

2. In American religion the emphasis is upon a *personal* experience that overrides everything else. *"In the 18th century, it was possible for individuals to find the form of religion that best suited their inclinations. By the 19th century, religious bodies had to compete in a consumer's market and grew or declined in terms of changing patterns of individual religious tastes"* (McCullough, 22).

3. This cancerous religious individualism is best portrayed by a study which quotes a young nurse, Sheila Lawson. She describes her faith as "Sheilaism." *"I believe in God. I'm not a religious fanatic. I can't remember the last time I went to church. My faith has carried me a long way. It's Sheilaism. Just my own little voice"* (Bellah, 221).

4. This devotion to individualism has brought chaos to our society. Morality, application of laws, personal responsibility, etc., have all become subject to individualism. Nowhere is this tragedy more evident than in religion.

   a. It introduced a cafeteria style religion – religion where devotees can pick and choose what is best for them and reject anything that is seen as *impractical* or *undesired.*

   b. It encourages the individual to "invite Jesus into your heart" and has developed an entire theology on "personal acceptance" that is swapped for the biblical call to surrender self to Jesus.

   c. It has created individual gods that fit our individual moods. A god who, in any way, threatens our comfort, our liberties, and our self-centered

9

lifestyles is not acceptable. We seek a god who will be tolerant of everything, condemning of nothing, and demanding of only the pleasurable.

Conclusion

I. ⌖ Have you ever considered that Exodus 20:4-5 was NOT addressed to pagans but to those who believed in God? A good friend of mine recently made a genuine confession about his concept of God: "I'm preaching through Exodus and last week's lesson was from 32:26-28. I really thought of skipping that passage because it portrays God in a way that I don't like. I was forced to see a side of God that causes me to recoil; I was very uncomfortable. But I really had no choice, did I?"

Modern minds look for a god that is most *needed* in their individual lives. It is proposed that we need a "holistic view of reality" and this requires new "models" of God. The resulting belief system seeks to allow each to find an image of god that works for them. ⌖ *"What God really is shouldn't concern us; what matters is finding an image of God that will be useful"* (McFague, 30). (Note: McFague proudly challenges Christians' usual speech about God as a sovereign monarch. She suggests three alternative possible metaphors for God – as mother, lover, and friend).

II. Here is a frank analysis of why Believers today are often guilty of forsaking the God of the Bible for other gods. ⌖ We have lost a sense of awe in appearing before the Almighty. ⌖ We fail to deal with God's silence when information is exploding around us. ⌖ We have been born and bred to reverence individualism more than we reverence God. The tragedy of making God into OUR image is illustrated by Israel's later history. The nation did not learn the lesson at Sinai of the damning folly of redesigning God to fit personal whims. Idolatry continually plagued the nation until God would excuse it no longer. Finally, exile occurred. As Babylonian troops were marching the exiles away, Jeremiah composed Lamentations. His words underscore the folly of allowing one's imaginations to fashion God (see Lamentations 5:1-3a).

III.   This sets the basis upon which our other lessons will stand. Let us make sure we are not guilty of...

    ✓ Remaking God into our image of what we feel the divine Deity should be.

    ✓ Redefining God by the world's vocabulary.

Failure to honor the God of the Bible is essentially self-centeredness—sin! It is a choice to follow folly instead of wisdom (Proverbs 9:10).

---

[1] Only the mimeographed booklet is available from this class study and it does not have any reference to the author or other citation information. The personal references in the material indicate the author grew up in a Texas congregation. These references also indicate a deliberate agenda to persuade others that the exclusive God of Holy Scripture does not command the exclusive religion as taught in the New Testament. The author's conclusion is that we are free to fashion a "god" that agrees with our feelings and wishes. References to this class material will be "Notes" and then the lesson and page number. For example "Notes 1:7" refers to the class notes lesson one, page seven.

- 2 -

Making the God of MY Choice

(Isaiah 40:18-25)

Introduction

I.   The "Spectre of the Brocken" is a phenomenon seen on a certain mountain in Germany. At dawn you can stand on the topmost ridge and behold a colossal shadowy spectre moving on the summits of the distant hills. The ancients saw this and concluded that it was a supernatural god. Fear captured their hearts and religious fervor offered sacrifices to this god who appeared only for a brief time in the early morning hours.

In later years it was discovered that this spectre was in truth only the shadow of the one who stood on the summit. As the sun would rise, the person's shadow was projected upon the morning mists

13

and it would move as the excited spectator would nervously move trying to gain a better viewpoint.

This aptly illustrates how man's folly has awarded "deity" to those things which are a mere reflection of self. Such is the truth of idolatry. That which is ascribed to God is actually a mirrored reflection of self.

The folly of idolatry is that many never see this truth.

II.   At the beginning of the Ten Commandments is the sin of idolatry. In fact, the summary prohibition of the combined Ten Commandments is the divine edict forbidding idolatry! ☞ This is the "sin of sins": for once idolatry has begun, man's understanding of who God really is befuddles his religious beliefs and practices forever, the Truth of God is polluted, and all is lost! Idolatry remains man's greatest threat.

   A.   Modern man will not become an idolater in the sense of the pagan mythologies of the Greeks, Romans, and Norse. These bowed down to a material image crafted with hands from precious metals or sacred wood and rocks. ☞ Modern man is too far advanced for such primitive ignorance.

   B.   Modern man's lure into idolatry is much more subtle and much more deadly. This danger is succinctly stated: *"The essence of idolatry is the entertainment of thoughts about God that are unworthy of Him. It begins in the mind...The idolater simply imagines things about God and acts as if they were true"* (Tozer, 5).

   C.   ☞ Satan's evil scheme is not to get us to say "there is no God" but to say there is a DIFFERENT God than what we have learned that the Bible teaches. This scheme begins in our minds (2 Corinthians 10:5).

   D.   The success of this evil scheme is repeatedly found in Scripture and has subtly invaded our modern society. In fact, it is alarming to see just how successful Satan's scheme has been.

E.   🖰 The idolater today is not one who bows down before some image, but is one who has mentally modified the God of the Scriptures so that He is now more attractive, more tolerant, more permissive, more loving, less denouncing, less damning, and less restrictive. Modern idolatry accepts the biblical religion and the biblical God, BUT modifies each to suit personal tastes. The result...

✓   🖰 A religion of convenience but no conviction

✓   🖰 A god who is personal and up close but not the sovereign Lord

✓   🖰 Adherents who follow feelings rather than faith

In summary, it is a religion, a god, and a group of adherents who are totally different from that which you read in the Bible. And it ALL results from modern idolatry and there is a shocking tolerance—our sensitivities and sensibilities have been dull and calloused! We seldom are stirred to righteous anger. We blithely accept perverseness as the new religious norm.

III.   🖰 Exodus 5:2 presents a searching question for modern hearts. *Is 37: 16-20*
① 45:17   *① 42:20*
④ 46:1-9

How do you answer Pharaoh's query...WHO is God? As your mind's eye looks at God, what is seen?

🖰 Isaiah 40:18-25—Underscored by the prophet's words is the power and majesty of God. The exclusiveness of the one, true God is clear and we are told that mankind has been informed of this great God since creation. The exalted position of God and the insignificance of mortals (vs. 22-25) reveal that man is foolish when he tries to make anything comparable to God. Here is the divine attitude toward anyone who attempts to redesign the God of Scripture. These verses are *"withering sarcasm poured upon the infatuation of idol framers and worshipers"* (Vine, 94).

Isaiah's repeated question emphasizes the position of God—God can be compared with nothing! Here is the heart of genuine faith. God is incomparable. In our thoughts of God we must be careful to keep our minds focused on the necessity of this infinite separation. 🖰 To remake God in our minds so He becomes something that bridges this infinity is idolatry; to break this absolute distinction is blasphemy (Isaiah 55:8-9).

Our series is a sobering study. It forces us to ask and answer an uncomfortable query—⌐⊖ Am I guilty of idolatry?

Body

The Traits of Idolatry. A survey of Scripture reveals that idolatry is characterized by the following traits. Look at these traits. Observe how they characterize those who bow down to graven images but also those who redesign God in their mind.

I. ⊖ The Supernatural is recognized

The existence of God is not denied. In fact, there is a willing confession that mortals are dependent upon a supernatural force that is beyond them (Romans 1:21; Exodus 32:4b; 2 Timothy 3:1-5; 1 Kings 20:23). The admission of the supernatural is true of our modern society. ⊖ God is not denied, just redefined to be something that is totally different than in Scriptures.

II. ⊖ The biblical God is redesigned

Psalm 81:9; Isaiah 43:12—The word "strange" in the Scripture comes from the root which means "to turn aside from." The basic thought suggested is that of non-acquaintance or non-relatedness. One has taken the basic idea of something and has "turned aside" from the true meaning and fashioned something totally different!

Those who seek to redefine God to allow for their anti-scriptural and unbiblical tolerances forget that God has condemned the "strange." ("Do not be carried away by varied and strange teachings." Hebrews 13:9).

This bluntly refutes those who assert that we worship "[A]*a god who could make orangutans, rhinos, coo-coo birds, pelicans, and a host of other strange and unique creatures has to be a God who can at least tolerate, if not love STRANGE THINGS!...there needs to be a spirit of love and acceptance for the variety of human expression...love means letting others be themselves, express themselves as they feel the need"* (Notes 7:13).

Inspiration records the Divine charge that man is not to change what has been ordered by the Almighty's directives—"My son, fear (hold in dread; highly respect) the LORD...Do not associate with those who are given to change" (Proverbs 24:21; see also Proverbs 22:28; 23:10).

III.   It is selfishly motivated

Those who practice idolatry are motivated by selfish interests. They reject the God of Scripture because He does not interest their selfish yearnings.   In turning away from the true biblical Deity, they fashion a "god" who can co-exist with their selfishness (Amos 7:10-17; 3 John 9).

IV.   It is sincerely misconstrued

This is ironic because of the involvement of selfishness.   This *sincerity* is not truth but a delusion (2 Thessalonians 2:10b-11). Ignorant of the prodding of selfishness, the idolaters perform their religion sincerely but in opposition to God (Matthew 7:21-23; 1 Kings 18:28). This trait is evident in the culture of idolatry that pervades our day—"sincerity" seems to be the only criterion by which one's religious beliefs and practices are judged. If one is "sincere," then even the worst practices are allowed.

Listen to the thinking that has deluded our modern religious communities: *"Each of us will see God differently, and seek to worship Him differently. It is my belief that God has given to each of us a personality type that seeks to worship Him differently from other personality types...Our God enjoys spontaneous, loving, heart-felt responses of any nature as long as they are authentic"* (Notes 1:6).

However, the God of Scripture does *not* accept those whose governing principle in religion is sincerity (1 Kings 13:21; 18:27-29).   One may be very sincere but be very wrong in religious beliefs and practices (Romans 10:1-3; Acts 23:1; 26:9). ☝ One may be very sincere but be damned eternally (Matthew 7:21-23).

Sadly the religious teachings of today have fashioned an idolatrous philosophy that denies this biblical Truth that we have to follow God's revealed commands as stated by the Lord Christ Jesus in Matthew 7:21.

V.   ☝ The Truth of God is changed

This is consequential to redefining God. ☝ The only way the biblical God can be refashioned is by altering or ignoring the biblical Truth about Him (Romans 1:25; 2 Timothy 2:17-18; 3:8; 4:3, 4; Jeremiah 23:16). ☝ This aspect of idolatry is common in our modern day. Many say there is *no* absolute, intrinsic Truth. ☝ They claim that Truth is only what is real to the individual—only that which is meaningful to the individual and anything that is not meaningful is not "truth." Therefore, truth about the biblical God is only *individual.* What may be true to one is possibly false to others. One's concept of God is thus built upon an ever-changing foundation (Malachi 3:6).

VI.   ☝ Perplexity and inconsistency marks their practices and beliefs

Because they are not following Truth, they constantly change beliefs. ☝ This will lead them to be confronted with the inconsistencies in their belief system. In our post-modern world truth has become *plastic*. It can be refashioned to fit one's latest desires.

Such will not be able to prove all things; they are unable to test teachings in an *objective* manner. When asked to give answers to religious beliefs, they will be confused (Jeremiah 23:19). Why? Because they do not have a foundation of absolute Truth for their answers.

☝ This trait is found in Psalm 97:7. The terms "confounded" (KJV) or "ashamed" (NASB) come from the Hebrew word בּוֹשׁ *(BOSH)*. This term means "to be ashamed; put to shame; disappointed." The primary meaning is "to fall into disgrace through failure, either of self or of an object of trust." *"Involved here are all the nuances of confusion, disillusionment, humiliation, and brokenness...The prophets normally use the word with this sense, promising Israel that unless she repents of her ways and turns from her idolatrous ways, she will certainly experience the shame of defeat and exile...Intimately associated...is the question of trust. If Israel seeks to insure her own glory by refusing to trust in God but rather trusts in idols (Isaiah 1:29), she will not get glory, but shame and disgrace"* (Harris, 97).

Modern idolaters are characterized by this trait. When asked about beliefs, they either get upset for being asked or try to explain with irrational feelings instead of confident facts. Their departure from the biblical God brings them to shame. Ultimately they become upset because they are asked to give a reason. They prefer to be left alone with their idolatry, never confronted (1 Peter 3:15).

VII. Quickly identified

Those who reject the biblical concept of God can be quickly identified by those who use the Scriptures (2 Timothy 3:8-9). There is a clear and unquestioned difference because of one's belief about God (1 Kings 22:7).

VIII. Stubbornness makes religion restricted

The only reason one rejects the biblical concept of God is to follow self. When we refuse to crucify self (Luke 9:23) we will submit to our selfish desires (i.e. *resentment* is a good illustration of this evil).

This selfishness soon redesigns God so that one feels he has divine approval (1 Samuel 15:23; Jeremiah 23:17; Leviticus 10:1-3). The selfish person looks at the biblical teaching regarding God, but he does not like what he sees. He then whittles upon the biblical concept until a more appealing god is found. This stubbornness fuels the individualism that feeds idolatry. Modern man seeks to find God in his own way; by his own experience; with his personal meaning. When one is told that God is not individually tailored to personal tastes, the stubborn heart balks (Acts 26:14)!

19

Conclusion

I.   ⌒ Leviticus 19:4 is God's command to be strong against the temptation to construct a god that fits my personal tastes—one that is comfortable for my lifestyle choices and one that is convenient when needed but at other times is conveniently tucked away and of no concern during the non-religious activities of my life.

This temptation has swayed mankind ever since Eden. But it is false doctrine and its evil brings damnation. It is rebuked with clarity by God's simple statement, "I AM THE LORD YOUR GOD."

"I am" refers to His eternal presence and His never-ending existence. He does not change. This means that the Truth regarding the God of the Bible is never altered. Fashions will constantly change, color schemes will come and go, man's concepts will always be fluid, but the God of the Bible remains exactly the same and never changes.

II.   How do you view God?

Someone once said to me, "That's my grandmother's god; the god of the past generation. That picture just doesn't work for me—I need something more." And so he constructed a god of his choice and individual tastes; one who was non-judgmental, non-threatening, non-restrictive but all-inclusive—it was a comfortable god. But it was not the God of the Scriptures. He worshiped his god, served his god, gave money to his god, and prayed to his god. But it was not the God of the Scriptures. On the Judgment Day he will bow before the God of the Scriptures and he will profess to have served, worshiped, and honored the *only* God but he will hear a startling statement—"Depart, I NEVER knew you!" (Matthew 7:21-23). It will be a great tragedy all because he practiced idolatry (Leviticus 26:30).

III.   How do you view God? (Isaiah 40:17-25)

    ✓ ⌒ Is it a negotiable portrait?

    ✓ ⌒ Is it crafted to personal tastes?

✓ ✍ Is it according to the Truth of the Scriptures?

We may not like certain aspects of God presented in the Scriptures. We may not like the emphasis upon God's rules, laws, and commands. We may not like the fact that the God of Scripture is the Sovereign and thus has a right to demand that we do some things and not do other things.

It does not matter what you or I like or dislike about God. God *IS* and He will not change. He is the "great I AM." All we can do is accept Him as He is and obey His will (1 John 5:21). No other choice!

The reality is that modern man has not accepted the simple description of God in the Scriptures. Modern minds have crafted a pantheon of gods. The members of this group are popular in the lives of modern men. Sadly, some Believers have redesigned the biblical God to occupy a position in this group. Our next lesson will begin examining some of the more popular gods who have been redesigned.

- 3 -

Believing Modern Idolatry's Lie

(1 Kings 12-13)

Introduction

I.   The topic of our discussion is "Believing a Lie." 🖱 Those seeking to redesign God and refashion the divine commands are required to offer support for their evil. They have to offer an alternative to what has been taught from the Scriptures. 🖱 Their offered alternative has to be cloaked in believable language and validated with believable authority. Notice how this process is discovered in the gold calf event.

Religious actions were performed. Religious language was used. Religious leaders were in charge. 🖱 It was all *religious* but all was *religious blasphemy*! Every word, action, attitude and position of the leaders was contrary to the Lord God Almighty. BUT the nation was led to do evil.

The tragic consequence was that all were sincere and excited and happy and exhilarated (Exodus 32:18) BUT it led to damnation! The worship was very moving and meaningful, BUT it was an affront to the Lord God Almighty. It did not

23

evidence devout worship in reverence and awe but a selfish attitude and complete rejection of God's commands.

At the foot of Sinai, the Israelites belief in a lie propelled them to turn toward the crudely fashioned gold calf—a series of lies were voiced and when left unchallenged these lies became beliefs.

🖰 Look at the lies that we find that were believed and left unchallenged:

A. "Come, make us a god who will go before us" (32:1).

B. "As for this Moses, we do not know what has become of him" (32:1).

C. Aaron fashioned it with a graving tool and made it into a molten calf; and said, "This is your god, O Israel, who brought you up from the land of Egypt" (32:4).

D. Aaron built an altar and made a proclamation and said, "Tomorrow shall be a feast to the LORD" (32:5).

E. Aaron said, "I said to them, 'Whoever has any gold, let them tear it off.' So they gave it to me, and I threw it into the fire, and out came this calf" (32:24).

Do you read the authority upon which this idolatry rested? It was "us," "we," "you," and "they." The authority was from man and *not* God; the leader (Aaron) permitted this to continue and even encouraged it!

🖰 This is the authority of modern idolatry. It is not founded upon the commands of God in the Bible but upon selfishness; and it is sanctioned by leadership that is focused more on pleasing man than upon pleasing God.

In our modern culture we will not be asked to throw in our gold rings and necklaces (modern man is too greedy to give up the treasures). 🖰 However, modern man will be asked to subscribe to actions, attitudes, expressions, emotions and other aspects that will make worship and God "more meaningful, exhilarating and pleasing." The process by which the modern worshipper is led to idolatry takes the same path as did ancient Israel at Sinai. We just modify things so the appeal is updated!

But it all revolves around "believing a lie." Before people will throw aside the commands of God they have to be presented with an alternative belief. This is found in persuading people to accept the validity of the alternative and then accept the alternative itself. After that, the gold calf is fashioned and idolatrous worship has begun!

How sad that the enlightened modern mind continues to be discontented with the revealed authority of Scripture and must redesign, rethink and refashion the commands of Scripture so they become more meaningful. This blasphemous attitude is pinpointed by Paul's inspired words to Timothy:

"For men will be lovers of self, lovers of money, boastful, arrogant, revilers, disobedient to parents, ungrateful, unholy, unloving, irreconcilable, malicious gossips, without self-control, brutal, haters of good, treacherous, reckless, conceited, lovers of pleasure rather than lovers of God, holding to a form of godliness, although they have denied its power...always learning and never able to come to the knowledge of the truth...so these men also oppose the truth, men of depraved mind, rejected in regard to the faith...their folly will be obvious to all" (2 Timothy 3:2-9).

II. The golden calf incident is not the only biblical text that warns against the disastrous ruin of believing lies and allowing lies to direct our response in worship and life to God. The essence of lying is selfishness. This is where lying and idolatry find a common connection: all is motivated by self-interests!

A. It is a very popular idea that it makes little difference in religious matters what a man believes as long as he is sincere and lives by his convictions. It is common in our modern times to hear people say that it does not matter what expressions are used in worship or what ethics guide our businesses as long as sincerity is evident.

25

5-16

A quote cited earlier in this series illustrates this god of utilitarian purpose: ⚆ *"What God really is shouldn't concern us; what matters is finding an image of God that will be useful"* (McFague, 30).

So, modern idolatry is actually a mimicking of the idolatry of the gold calf event—all is focused on ME; all expressions are for ME; all is designed to give ME exhilaration and a "holy WOW!"

The determining question is not what does God command and what is decent and orderly. The determining question is, "How can we design all events in the worshipping assembly to be a production rivaling with Broadway theatrics!"

The shift has changed from God to ME!

Our consciences hold us guilty unless any worship/religious response to God has biblical foundation (at least MOST still have a conscience seeking biblical support. But even today this is fading and all that remains is Self's directives). Hence, we hear the advocates for any worship expression, or any act that leads to encouragement, and inclusion of any sincere person as long as we agree upon one point (the "god of our cause"). As long as these have a smattering of support from any biblical text, many feel comfortable in allowing such. But it is a LIE! Believing a lie is not a matter of small concern to God.

B. ⚆ A biblical Truth that the majority chooses to ignore: God is a God who looks at the *small things*! Modern idolatry urges its followers to accept the teaching, "God doesn't sweat the small stuff." This is a flagrant lie! God has always urged strict obedience to the small details in life, worship, and personal morality. Look at the minute details God gave regarding the construction of the Tabernacle. He was very concerned about the small things!

For emphasis, let me repeat: ⚆ It is a very popular idea that it makes little difference in religious matters what a man believes as long as he is sincere and lives by his convictions. It is common in our modern times to hear people say that it does not matter what expressions are used in worship or what ethics guide our businesses. This is comforting. This is all-inclusive. This results in "warm-fuzzies" for everyone. But it is evil error!

C. This is a very damaging philosophy. While applying it to religion, no one would dare apply it to other matters. The governing of religious doctrines found in the Bible is given to us by the Almighty God so we will live good lives. Accept the biblical teachings and follow them and you will find joy (Proverbs 2:1-22). If one accepts the biblical teachings and then redesigns and modifies them, they will find terror (Matthew 7:21-23).

The very suggestion that one would compartmentalize the biblical teachings in one area and apply a different reasoning to their practices (than applied to the practices of daily life) is absurd.

1. One would not place savings in an institution which is corrupt and not lose money. No amount of sincerity would cause the management to be honest.

2. A young woman is engaged to a man with deceitful motives. Will her sincerity prevent her from a lifetime of misery which is sure to come?

3. The belief of a lie has caused the defeat of many a brave army and the sinking of many a gallant ship.

D. It is indeed strange that one would state that this principle is harmless in the religious realm!

III. There are three passages of Scripture that speak clearly on our subject. A proper discussion of each will show the fallacy of following the philosophy of "sincerity is sufficient!"

A. 2 Thessalonians 2:10-12

B. 1 Kings 12, 13

C. Matthew 15:14

IV. ⟡ In order to focus on this lesson, it is important to define exactly what we mean by the term "lie" as used in the sense of a religious lie regarding beliefs and doctrines. A rule of thumb would be to ask, "If the belief of a lie leads one to sin or fail to do ALL that is commanded by God, in the way God directs, it will prove fatal unless forgiven by God!"

Body

I. ⟡ Look at **2 Thessalonians 2:10-12**.

A. The context of the passage is directed to the very point of this lesson. A congregation of God's People is being threatened with apostasy. Someone was bringing them damnable lies dressed like sheep! It sounded like biblical teaching. It was being advocated by religious leaders. ⟡ BUT it was a damning lie (Matthew 7:15-20).

1. The man of lawlessness was described (verses 3-10a). He is the focal point of those seeking to invade and compromise God's People.

2. Notice that in verse 10b attention is switched from the man to those who are being misguided by this deceiver.

    a. The main instrument of this person is deceit (verse 10a)!

    b. ⟡ Because they are deceived, they are perishing!

B. There is a clear application of this passage to our lesson.

1. ⟡ God did not make these people believe a life by direct pressure. They had a choice. ⟡ They had been taught God's Truth. ⟡ They were obligated to guard this Truth and hold fast to its teachings. God allowed them to be worked upon by error until they were enveloped by a false security. ⟡ God allowed them a personal choice. To whom will they be committed? To what doctrine will they submit?

2. The result of believing a lie is **not** salvation, but condemnation; and that condemnation will be eternal unless one obtains God's forgiveness (verse 12).

   The deciding criterion was pleasure. They were seeking to please self rather than God! Such is diametrically opposite to what is demonstrated by those committed to the Lord God Almighty (Galatians 6:14). How terribly sad it is to observe that this pleasure is dominating choices in modern society and modern religion!

3. The natural consequences of a lie are injurious, especially when it leads one away from the love of the Truth.

4. In verse 12 Paul connects believing a lie with the failure to love the Truth and with taking pleasure in unrighteousness. So deluded are these people that instead of enjoying God's Truth they enjoy a lie! These have convinced themselves that it is a "small thing" that is commanded and that God is not concerned with the small things. So they casually brush aside all teachings that are inconvenient!

II.   🖰 1 Kings 12, 13

A. These chapters present us with one of the most amazing narratives of the entire Bible. Yet it is seldom the basic text of sermons, devotionals, or Bible classes. The narrative reveals shocking truths that are associated with this series discussing how modern man redesigns and rethinks God and so makes God in his own image. Look at the story and highlight these points of particular interest.

1. A young prophet is sent to rebuke Jeroboam in Bethel as the apostate King begins the idolatrous worship that will cement the division of the Israelite Kingdom. Clear commands from God were given and specific obedience was expected. There was no mistaking the will of God.

2. The prophet arrives just as the King was about to light the first incense (13:1).

3. The events that transpired convinced the King that the prophet was God-sent.

4. The King offers refreshments to the prophet, but the refreshments are refused (13:9). The reason these refreshments were refused was clearly given—God said "NO!" Some today would compromise and interpret this as a message from God to forego the prior commands. Some today would shrug off the prohibition saying that "God never told me what to do if the King offered food and drink. Since God was silent on this I can do it." Some today would depreciate the clear commands from God saying that this gives an opportunity to join another who feels like we do—inclusion instead of exclusion!

One can look at this situation and arrive at his own understanding, but there are no confusing directives about what God commanded and expected.

We are obligated to practice "understanding" in our responses to God's commands (Psalm 32:9a; 49:20; 111:10; Proverbs 2:11; 3:5; Jeremiah 4:22).

5. An old prophet heard of the news and tricked the young prophet into dining with him (13:18, 19).

   a. He was a recognized religious leader. He was respected, honored and above question.

   b. He based his words upon a foundation of God's revelation.

   c. He presented an alternative to what the young prophet had heard from God.

   d. He was convincing.

e. "BUT, he lied to him" (verse 18b). 🖰 The young prophet believed a lie. The young man was sincere. He believed in God. He was on a mission to obey God. He had been faithful in his duty UNTIL he believed a lie!

6. 🖰 Because of believing a lie, he was killed (13:24). 🖰 Nothing mattered...his sincerity did not matter; his faithfulness to prior duty did not matter; his belief in God did not matter. 🖰 What mattered was that he did not obey God because he was told a lie and he followed a lie instead of Truth.

He knew Truth. He had agreed to follow Truth. He had upheld his loyalty to Truth in the face of the King. He had been faithful in so much and had only failed in this *small matter*. But he was killed. 🖰 Do not allow the inescapable application of this fact to be overlooked.

Yes, it was a horrible tragedy. Yes, it was unfair for the young prophet to be treated that way by the old prophet. Yes, the young prophet was duped and deceived. But he was killed. Believing a lie was catastrophic.

B. Observations from this account

1. At the beginning, the young prophet was to be admired.

a. For his courage to God, he defied the powers of the King.

b. For his freedom from ambition, he resisted flattery from the King.

c. For his unselfishness, he was not influenced by the King's money.

2. Yet this man was a failure to God and himself.

a. Even though he was good and brave, he was overcome.

b. There will be many a good and brave person on the Day of Judgment who will be lost because of believing a lie! (Matthew 7:21-23).

c. Perhaps you say that the sin of the old prophet was just as wrong, or more so, than that of the young prophet. But you cannot justify disobedience to God by pointing to another instance of disobedience. BOTH were sinners. The old prophet was evil, but the young prophet had the Word of God and should have trusted God's Word instead of mortal's philosophy. The world needed a lesson on the dangers of believing a lie as much as on lying (verse 26).

d. 🖱 Romans 15:4 was written not to warn us about lying, but about *believing* a lie.

III. Consider now the third text, 🖱 **Matthew 15:14**

A. Our Lord's words teach the same point that Paul and the historian of 1 Kings taught on the subject of being condemned by believing a lie.

1. The very cause of falling into the ditch was blindness.

2. Applied in a spiritual sense, this passage supports even clearer our thesis.

3. Ignorance due to misguidance results in a vast majority falling away and being lost.

B. 🖱 The greatest danger that is present in today's irreligious culture is to be lost because one blindly follows a religious guide or person and forsakes the Scriptures (1 John 4:1).

Conclusion

I. 🖱 After looking at these three texts, we should remember the tragedy that is waiting for those who continue to believe and practice religious lies.

A. Some will contend that we do not know the Truth on every subject and should not condemn others for believing a certain way. This is true in matters of opinion, NOT faith. 🖱 In matters of faith, God HAS given us the instructions required (2 Peter 1:3). God HAS clearly expressed what the Divine commands are and that obedience to all is required if one follows God in sincerity.

⌙ God HAS clearly expressed that the boundaries of our religious expressions, beliefs, and commands are those revealed in Scripture and that one should NOT "go beyond what has been written" (1 Corinthians 4:6).

B. A rule of thumb guarding our religious activities and beliefs might be stated in these words, "If the belief of a lie leads one to sin or hinders him from proper obedience to God or allows that which God has not commanded or it diminishes the reverence and awe that belongs to God, it will prove fatal unless confessed, repented and forgiven by God!"

C. Any kind of religious lie that will cause one to sin and fall short of doing God's will is the type of lie which will condemn a soul to hell and rob it of a blissful crown.

⌙ It is morally **inexcusable** to persuade people to believe and follow religious lies. ⌙ It is morally **reprehensible** for one to be aware another is following a religious lie and remain silent.

⌙ Will we sit in silence and permit people to press their religious lies? Will we silently sit and refuse to confront religious lies?

II. ⌙ How can we be sure that we are not being led by false guides?

A. ⌙ We must allow only those who can see to direct us (Acts 17:11).

B. There is only one group of men qualified -- those inspired of God and those who related His commands and will to mankind via the Holy Bible (1 Thessalonians 2:13).

C. ⌙ We should not listen to any man, accept any teachings, or follow any tradition that cannot be found in THE BOOK! Otherwise, we may be like the young prophet. We may be led to believe a lie and, thereby, lose our own soul (Galatians 1:8).

III.   The Father of all lies continues to delude many today through lies he perpetrates through human beings.

   A. ☝ There is one lie which has been taught wherever the gospel has gone—There is time enough yet!

      1. Under its fatal delusion, millions die without God and without hope.

      2. Under its delusion, multitudes of Christians excuse themselves from working in the Lord's vineyard.

   B. ☝ Sincerity is not sufficient for salvation. To be saved one must be sincere; but one must also complete obedience to God's Will (Matthew 7:21).

   C. Will you resolve to conform to the Truth instead of lies?

Source: some of the basis for this lesson came from a written sermon by J.W. McGarvey.

- 4 -

A Pantheon of gods

(Isaiah 40:18-25)

Introduction

I. The triumph of the Gospel over paganism in the Swedish north lands is punctuated with a number of intriguing stories:

King Olaf of Norway once faced a group of pagan farmers who were armed and prepared for war. A meeting was called and Olaf exhorted the farmers to accept the true God and put away their idols.

"Gudbrand, the chief of the place, answered, 'We know nothing of him thou speakest about. Do you call him a God whom no one can see? We have a god that we should have brought to the assembly to-day, but that it is so rainy; and the sight of him will make your blood run cold.'

"It was arranged that if the morrow should be fair, the idol should be brought, and after a further explanation they would either do as the king desired or else fight him.

🖱 *"This god was Thor the Thunderer. Every day five cakes were set before him and as they disappeared, he was believed to have consumed them. The next day was favorable" (Foster, 480).*

The two armies grouped together on either side of a great plain. Olaf with his attendant, Grimkel, approached the chief. The pagan multitude parted as a great image, gleaming with silver and gold, was carried on the shoulders of men. It was set down in the midst of the field.

"The heathen chief stood up and said, 'Where now, O king, is your God? I think he will be abashed before this glorious god of ours, whom I see you fear.'

"Then King Olaf arose and answered, 'Much hast thou talked, and greatly hast thou wondered, because thou canst not see our God; but we expect his arrival. Thou wouldst frighten us with thy blind and deaf god, who cannot move and must be borne upon your shoulders. But now,' he cried aloud, 'look to the east, behold, our God, is coming!'

"All looked that way, and at that instant Kolbing, a faithful servant of the king, smote the idol with a large club, as previously instructed. The fragments of the terrific god were scattered on all sides, and out came a great swarm of rats and mice. The Pagans fled in all directions.

"The king rose and said, 'You see yourselves what your god can do—the idol you adorned with gold and silver, and to which ye offered meat. Take now your gold and ornaments from the grass and give them to your wives and daughters; but never hang them hereafter on stocks and stones.'

"He then offered them the alternative of accepting Christianity or fighting his army. To fight was folly, and the Pagans sullenly submitted and were baptized by the pope. Thus was idolatry put away in the eleventh century!" (Foster, 481).

II.   Our series is asking a very sobering question—🖱 Am I guilty of idolatry?

A. Not necessarily bowing down and offering cakes to Thor, but are you taking the biblical God and modifying Him to be something different than what He is in the Bible. Such is a startling thought.

🖱 Idolatry seems too ancient and too ignorant to be practiced today. 🖱 But it is widely practiced. Even Christians are guilty of practicing idolatry!

"Idolatry is worshiping anything that ought to be used, or using anything that ought to be worshiped" (Augustine).

B. The idea of dealing with idolatry is presented in some devotional thoughts:

"Years ago I was talking to a guy who was bragging about his wealth and detailing all the many ways God had blessed him. The guy had built a successful business that he was quite proud of. He described how much his profits had increased in the past five years and boasted about the value of his company. He told me about his second home in the ski resort of Aspen, Colorado, and the private jet he used for business trips and to shuttle his family back and forth on their frequent, exotic vacations.

Finally, I felt compelled to challenge him just a little bit. "You said that God blessed you. Do you feel any responsibility to use what God has given you to make a difference?" I fully expected him to soften, maybe even to backtrack and tell me about someone he had helped, perhaps describe some ministry or charity he supported financially. Maybe he hadn't wanted to brag about his giving or to reveal ways God had led him to invest in the kingdom. But the guy steamrolled ahead and calmly explained why he didn't feel compelled to give.

Dumbfounded, I asked him to clarify. "You mean you don't give anything? Like, nothing at all?"

Then he said something I'll never forget. Without reservation, he replied, "I don't give anything away because I love money. Love making it. Love spending it. Love what it buys. I love how it makes me feel. I earn my own money, so I use it on myself. Period." I imagine my jaw must have hit the floor, because then he added, "And don't go telling me how the love of money is the root of all evil. I've heard that before. That may be true for some people, but God and I are fine. He blesses me, and it's mine to spend the way I want. This is the way I am, and I'm not changing."

In the Old Testament, Gideon faced a similar problem with the people around him. They willingly bowed to idols and thumbed their noses at God in the process. But God was having none of it. With righteous passion, he told Gideon, Tear down your father's altar to Baal and cut down the Asherah pole beside it (Judges 6:25).

Notice that God didn't tell Gideon to help the people manage their idols, to shorten them by a few feet, just keep them under control. No, He commanded Gideon to tear them down. Cut down the poles.

Don't tolerate the idols. Crush them. Destroy them. Smash them. Obliterate them.

Gaining the better requires tearing down the idol. Don't manage it. Destroy it."

(Groeschel, *Devotionals Daily*. February 6, 2016).

C. A common practice of modern idolatry is to redesign the God of the Bible so that He becomes more comfortable to the individual's belief system, life's choices and behaviors. Here are a few of these redesigned gods.

Body

I.   🖰 **The God of MY Cause.**

A. Many today are involved in critical causes. We live in a time when almost every aspect of culture seems unstable and some group is trying to restore that stability. Of course, in whatever cause one supports it is *that* cause that is most important and *that* cause which deserves the best support. Who else is a better support for *my* cause than the Almighty God? If God is a part of *my* cause then I cannot lose!

B. ⌐ **The problem:** This thinking depreciates God by making the Cause larger than God. The Cause begins to dictate God's approval, etc. The end result (the triumph of the Cause) is the object of devotion!

C. In society this has been seen as God becomes the "Heavenly Champion" for oppressed nations, the feminist agenda, the ecological propaganda, carnal wars, etc. In case after case, the God of the Bible is redefined so as to serve the Cause. ⌐ The end result—the Sovereign becomes the Slave! What is seldom admitted is that the cause was prompted because of selfish interest and self-fashioned an appropriate idol to help give supernatural help to our cause!

D. This revamping of God has led to the modern concepts of the God of the Bible being models of the Divine Mother, the Divine Lover, and the Divine Friend.

E. *"What God really is shouldn't concern us; what matters is finding an image of God that will be useful"* (McFague, 30).

F. 1 Samuel 4:3-8 illustrates this kind of idolatry. God is used to support a Cause. His deity was limited and changed by man's idolatry.

G. This "god of MY cause" is an amazing thing. He will unite me with those holding contrary beliefs on everything EXCEPT on the one Cause for which I modify God to champion. Such strange alliances reveal the self-centeredness of this form of idolatry; union exists for just one purpose! (Mark 3:6).

H. We must be careful lest we allow some cherished Cause lead us into idolatry where we compromise many doctrines just so we will agree upon one (1 John 5:21).

II. ⌐ **The God of MY Understanding.**

A. Some commit idolatry by restricting God to the way *we* want Him to operate; the doctrines *we* want Him to stress.

B. 🖰 In this idolatry we draw fellowship by the criteria *we* like.

Often in drawing such lines, we force God to condone/condemn what Self prompts. Such is illustrated in the multitude of religious creeds/confessions that divide the world. What started as a well-intended act results in imprisoning God and deluding ourselves. 🖰 The practical impact—

- 🖰 WE decide what is important.

- 🖰 WE force God to subscribe to our list.

- 🖰 WE believe that God feels very much at home in the list and is "not comfortable" with anyone who does not subscribe to our list!

🖰 This produces an "arrogant certainty" by which idolatry is practiced (Matthew 23:2-4) and awaits God's harsh condemnation (Matthew 23:13-33).

C. 🖰 The basic problem—

- 🖰 WE limit God by what WE want to understand the Bible to command and teach!

- 🖰 We define "God" in the way WE want to understand Him (1 Kings 20:23).

D. Many today understand God only in terms of *grace* or *love* because they do not want to understand Him in any other way. Once they step back and examine the god they have redesigned, they find that he is too trivial to be worth the effort. (If God is all grace, no law, then why be concerned about godly living? Why insist that anyone obey the gospel?).

E. The only way to find the true God is to possess understanding of ALL the Scripture says about Him (Ephesians 1:17-18; Colossians 1:9). A rigid catechism or a permissive faith only erects idols and never provides a true understanding of God.

F. ✋ The god of MY understanding proclaims: *"We need to express joy* (Notes 6:2)...*God is happy with each individual's efforts to worship Him...I might not appreciate the method by which another human honors and glorifies God, but I'm not God and I cannot speak for Him. A god who could make orangutans, rhinos, coo-coo birds, pelicans, and a host of other strange and unique creatures has to be a God who can at least tolerate, if not love STRANGE THINGS!...there needs to be a spirit of love and acceptance for the variety of human expression...love means letting others be themselves, express themselves as they feel the need"* (Notes 7:13). Heb 13:9
Psalm 144

III.   ✋ **The God of MY Experience.**

A. This is one of the most favorite idols in religion today. Mankind places feelings and experiences as the ultimate god. ✋ The God of the Bible is thus defined by MY experiences—if I feel it, it must be true! ✋ This is the epitome of an uncontrolled *individualism.*

B. ✋ This idol is very destructive because it allows the subjective to mold the spiritual and ignore the objective revelation (Scripture). It is often phrased, "I know what the Bible teaches, but I feel about it differently!"

C. ✋ This idol seduces us to change God's commands in critical areas. *"'Some of us were wondering whether it is really possible to worship God in this church.' I knew what she wanted, but I forced her to stammer it out: she wanted a particular style of worship, a more intense emotional experience with certain praise choruses and speaking in tongues. Anything other than this, in her thinking, could not be genuine worship"* (McCullough, 35).

D. ✋ For some this "god of MY experience" becomes the only standard of authority in religion (2 Kings 17:28-33).

✋ Those who idolize this god are constantly whining for the exciting, the sensational, and the goose-bump religion but fail to find the security of objective faith in an absolute God. They bounce from one experience to another; from

41

boredom to sensation back to boredom. For them worship/service to the biblical God is never satisfying (2 Timothy 3:2-9).

Conclusion

I. ⚐ We have discussed three "gods" idolized by our modern mind. Such redesigns of the Almighty God will provide comfort for our Causes, security in our beliefs, and assurance in our experiences BUT will never provide the contented peace that passes all understanding.

   A. ⚐ If I worship the *"god of MY Cause"* I will live life inconsistently and will wander from Cause to Cause and force God to fit my agenda instead of crucifying Self and accepting God's commands (Philippians 4:1-6).

   B. If I worship the *"god of MY Understanding"* I will limit the Almighty God to what I want Him to be and will never find the freedom that comes from knowing the whole Truth of God (John 8:31-32).

   C. If I worship the *"god of MY Experiences"* I will forever live enslaved to emotions or sensations and will never know the absolute security that is provided to those who follow Scripture (1 John 5:13).

II. ⚐ Isaiah 17:7—Mortals have no choice but to "have regard" for the Almighty God revealed in Scripture. This word refers to a steady gaze because one is very interested. *"It is never a casual or disinterested glance...Isaiah 17:7-8. God says that the time is coming when a 'man will regard his maker' and no more have regard for the altars which his hands have made"* (Harris, 944).

In such times mankind will be concerned only in what the Scripture says about the Almighty God. ⚐ In such times personal crusades, understanding, and experiences are never allowed to redefine God's commands and the divine will for man's behavior. In such times the honest Believer joins young Samuel and pliantly says, "Speak Lord for Your servant is listening" (1 Samuel 3:9).

- 5 -

The Pantheon Increases

(Isaiah 40:18-25)

Introduction

I. A missionary in Sierra Leone called on a heathen widow and was surprised at the evidences of paganism in the home. She had in her room four gods—one for herself, one for her husband, and one for each of her two children. She had been rubbing *eggiddi* (a rich food paste made of corn flour mixed with palm oil) on the idols' mouths, but they did not eat. The missionary tried to show the woman the folly of her act, but she would not listen. 🖰 She was "joined to her idols!"

Hosea 4:17 shows this problem: "Ephraim is joined to idols; let him alone."

"Joined" is from בַר (chăbar khaw-bar'). This is from a primitive root that means *to join* (literally or figuratively); specifically (by means of spells) to *fascinate*. Such has been charmed to the extent he is joined together in an unquestioned league or union. In this sense, ancient Israel had been so charmed by the idols that she refused to question her situation; she was fascinated. The Almighty God had become less appealing and easily replaced!

II.   Idolatry has always plagued mankind. Man has seldom been content to worship/serve God according to God's directions. ⚐ He has always wanted to modify the divine decrees in some ways.

Even in the New Testament dispensation the allurement of idolatry continues to entice man to devise a modified version of the Almighty (Acts 15:19-20). ⚐ Those who redesign God are "polluted." Use of this term indicates that in turning to a concept of God, other than that presented by revelation, corrupts the purity of religion (Deuteronomy 4:16).

Our modern campaigns against pollution of the ecosystem follow a carefully orchestrated strategy to show the putrid consequences of allowing self-centered desires to destroy the intricate balance of nature. This is exactly what happens with idolatry. The purity of religion devoted to the Almighty God is corrupted by self-centered desires. Just as a polluted ecosystem is repulsive, so is the polluted religious system.

⚐ When we make God in OUR image, we are corrupting a very delicate system. ⚐ Consequences will be catastrophic!

III.   The very suggestion that Christians in our enlightened era can be enticed to idolatry is shocking! We are confident that such will never happen to us. However, it is possible (1 Corinthians 10:12). Past lessons have revealed disturbing points:

A.   ⚐ The biblical awe and reverence for God has been lost in our day. We dare approach the Almighty God with a casual indifference—no sweaty palms, no shaky knees, no humble heart. A rabid individualism rules our religion and each feels comfortable to "find God in his own way." This situation existed at Mt. Sinai and brought doom (Exodus 32:1-4).

B.   ⚐ The practice of idolatry is not the bowing down to a graven image but is the result of our efforts to redesign the Almighty to become a god of individual tastes. Stubbornly this revamped god is worshiped and zealously defended as the divine advocate for self-centered faith (Jeremiah 23:16-19).

C. 🖰 Self-centered idolatry has designed a pantheon of gods that are well-suited to our individualism. We first looked at three individualized gods in the last lesson:

1. The god of *MY CAUSE* leads me to create a god who is used to promote one issue.

2. The god of *MY UNDERSTANDING* is the promoter of the one doctrine that I feel is important

3. The god of *MY EXPERIENCE* is the god that authorizes feelings to govern and sanction any and every desire.

D. We now examine three more gods of modern religion. Each shares a common point with all others—self-centeredness! 🖰 Hearts are unwilling for the Almighty God of the Bible to rule so He is redesigned and His doctrines are refashioned.

Body

I. The God of MY COMFORT.

A. 🖰 If there is one word which summarizes our present culture it is "comfort." We are living in times that worship must be *comfortable*. This dark longing is illustrated by our culture. Anything offering instant relief, soothing satisfaction or inner-peace is a best seller. From international coffees, to flavored teas, to St. John's Wort, to a myriad of over-the-counter medicines our society is seeking for comfort! Self-help books are the best sellers because they offer the definitive way to find comfort from obesity to boredom to laziness.

B. 🖰 If we can demand and receive comfort from fitness to diet programs, we think the same self-centered demands can be provided in religion.

C. *"At one time theologians argued that the chief purpose of humankind was to glorify God. Now it would seem that the logic has been reversed: the chief*

45

purpose of God is to glorify humankind. Spirituality no longer is true or good because it meets absolute standards of truth or goodness, but because it helps me get along. I am the judge of its worth. If it helps me find a vacant parking space, I know my spirituality is on the right track. If it leads me into the wilderness, calling me to face dangers I would rather not deal with at all, then it is a form of spirituality I am unlikely to choose" (Wuthnow, 1239-1240).

D. 🖰 Those in the world are enticed by a god of comfort. They want a religious "good-time god" who advocates "Do your own thing, the way YOU want! Eat, drink, and be merry—only have a good time with God!"

E. 🖰 Of course the biblical call for self-surrender (Luke 9:23; Galatians 2:20) must be changed in order for this "good-time god" to reign. So many seek to reach into the world by offering a cafe menu of religiously associated items in order to "meet felt-needs" of the community. *"Perhaps this is why we rarely hear the church speaking the language of conversion (e.g. 'born again,' 'new life in Christ'); instead its lingua franca is rehabilitation (e.g. 'renewed,' 'journeying toward wholeness,' 'discovering meaning'). Christian ministry has become an effort to help people cope with their problems well enough to find a bit of happiness"* (McCullough, 41-42).

F. 🖰 There is an interesting (but sad) point in this search for comfort. 🖰 The Almighty God is not ignored but is brought in to help; something like the "great Therapist" who can offer the right answer...IF He is properly invoked! Thus the God of Scriptures has become the therapeutic god offering the supreme comfort. Bowing before this god will help me get what I want!

G. People lured by this god of comfort come wanting to be happy and expecting God to make it so! Their "needs" are focused totally upon SELF; their "desires" and behaviors and life's choices are not seen as the problem—in fact these are dismissed, ignored, or excused! Such behaviors and lifestyles are evil sins; but no longer do we dare use the term "sin"!

H. How does this "god of comfort" harmonize with Scripture?

46

1. ☙ Matthew 4:1-11—If ever there was a passage that would support this philosophy, here it is! Whatever *god* promises to fulfill all of our desires is the devil in disguise!

2. Scripture teaches that Christians are not guaranteed comfort because of faith. In fact, Christians will find less comfort than those in the world (Luke 9:23; 2 Timothy 3:12; Philippians 1:20).

3. Isaiah 45:9—The idol to the god of therapy allows self to dictate its demands (needs) to the Almighty. It leads one to no longer follow God's Word (Scripture) but self-pacification!

I. ☙ If your chief goal is comfort/pleasure, it makes perfect sense to find a church where the god of comfort/pleasure is revered! ☙ If your church is concerned with drawing large numbers of those whose religion is based upon self-centeredness rather than self-sacrifice, it makes sense to offer the world this god of comfort! This was not an option in the 1st Century (1 Corinthians 1:18-29).

II. The God of MY SUCCESS.

A. ☙ If "comfort" is our culture's first priority, then "success" is a close second. We live in a culture that encourages a relentless yearning for success. The drive for success is so forceful that many are trapped on the treadmill of self-destruction. *"It's tough to climb the ladder of success, especially if you're trying to keep your nose to the grindstone, your shoulder to the wheel, your eye on the ball, and your ear to the ground"* (McCullough, 44). Because it is so tough, WE need some divine help and thus redesign the God of Scripture to become the god of MY success (the "Celestial Ringer," the "franchise player" who will guarantee success!).

B. We look at Matthew 7:7, 11 and our idolatrous wishes are made. ☙ We pray for success but instead of spiritual help we seek a Management Consultant, Financial Advisor, and Personal Trainer—all in One Mighty Being! ☙ The chief business of God becomes material prosperity (a revamped Genie in the bottle; but this time there are unlimited wishes!).

This idolatry is illustrated by those who take the prayer of Jabez (1 Chronicles 4:10) and wrest it to their selfish purposes. Here is a review regarding a book on the prayer of Jabez. Read carefully and notice how this philosophy plays to the "god of MY Success":

*"**The Prayer of Jabez: Breaking Through to the Blessed Life.** Is a timeless prayer that produces timely results! Bruce Wilkinson takes readers to 1 Chronicles 4:10 to discover how they can release God's miraculous power and experience the blessings God longs to give each of us. The life of Jabez...bursts...in an audacious, four part prayer that brings him an extraordinary measure of divine favor, anointing, and protection. Readers who commit to offering the same prayer on a regular basis will find themselves extravagantly blessed by God, and agents of His miraculous power...Do you want to be extravagantly blessed by God?*

"Are you ready to reach for the extraordinary? To ask God for the abundant blessings He longs to give you? Discover how the remarkable prayer of a little-known Bible hero can release God's favor, power, and protection. You'll see how one daily prayer can help you leave the past behind and break through to the life you were meant to live" (Book review on Amazon.com).

C. In 1990 over 50 Japanese computer engineers held a temple ceremony in which homage was paid to old computer chips that were presented to Buddha. The Shogun confidently said, "No doubt this reverence will pay off for the Japanese people."

D. 🖱 Acts 8:18—Simon illustrates the idolatry of the god of success.

E. 🖱 If material prosperity is your goal, it makes perfect sense for you to worship this god of success. 🖱 If you seek to relate to those in our culture who are worshiping this god of success, it makes perfect sense for the church to be presented in ways that will draw them!

F. 🖱 There is a big problem with this idol. Even when the god of success leads to prosperity, it cannot lead to happiness (1 Timothy 6:6-10); it cannot lead to salvation (Luke 18:18-25).

    1. 🖱 Ecclesiastes 2:1-11; 1 Kings 10:1-29—Solomon's god of success brought misery.

    2. Philippians 3:4-14—Paul found great success by turning to the biblical God!

G. 🖱 We need to redefine "success" instead of redefining God! (Joshua 1:6-9). *"The God who sent the beloved Son to reveal abundant life and let him die poor, powerless, and despised on a Roman cross has done precisely that: by declaring this death a victorious ending to a perfect life, God has not only redefined success for all time but has sent the god-of-my-success tumbling to the bottom of the ladder"* (McCullough, 46).

III. The God of MY NATION.

A. 🖱 Nationalistic gods have always deluded men. Even in our modern era these nationalistic gods continue to pose problems (Ireland; Lebanon; ISIS, etc.). 🖱 Satan often tempts us with an enticing idea that one particular nation has a divine destiny to fulfill. Such is painfully true in the United States of America.

B. 🖱 The United States of America has a national god that it holds as her Protector. A 1990 survey asked 113,000 Americans to identify their religion: 86% said Christian (by any reasoning this should make our nation one characterized by "Christian" behavior). Actual behavior suggests that our Christian heritage is only a sentimental preference rather than a deep commitment! A more recent survey reveals that in 2015 only 49% of Americans considered themselves as "Christians." Our nation has thus lost its renowned distinction as a "Christian nation" and has become a "secular nation."

C. The true soul of our nation is exposed in this: *"These are modern times. Nothing bad is going to happen to us. If we get fired, it's not failure; it's a mid-life vocational reassessment period. If we screw up a marriage, we can get another one. There's no shame in divorce. Day Care will take the kids, and the ex-wife can go back to [her career]...If we get convicted of a crime, we'll go to tennis prison...Or maybe we can join a support group and get off the hook by listening to shrinks tell us we don't like ourselves enough...play our cards right, and we can get a book contract out of it"* (O'Rourke, 121).

D. ⌘ In the United States of America today, God is draped in red-white-blue and it is believed this nation is on God's most favored list. What's good for America is good for God. So we legislate laws, loosen punishments, ignore morality and confidently worship the god of MY nation who agrees. It seems that many citizens believe there is little difference between the Kingdom of God and the United States of America. In the primaries, party caucuses, political conventions, the Congress and the White House this god of MY nation is revered and used to give supernatural consent to our self-centered lifestyles!

E. What does Scripture say? ⌘ Letting God define political commitments is one thing; but letting political commitments define God is idolatry! ⌘ When we allow the God of Scripture to be redesigned to fit our national crusades, we are sinning (1 Kings 12:26-33; 1 Kings 15:9-14; 2 Chronicles 16:7-10). ⌘ When nations reject the Sovereign, Almighty God of Scripture and replace Him with the god of their nation, misery results (2 Chronicles 28:23).

Conclusion

I. The Lord's Church has been more influenced by cultural trends than we want to admit. ⌘ To be frank, more Christians share a greater loyalty to cultural gurus than to the Lord Christ; a greater sympathy to society's feelings than to the Almighty; a greater commitment to Self's interests than to eternal priorities! These factors make a ready market for religious idols offering gods of individual tastes.

III. We have discussed four more "gods" idolized by our modern mind. Such redesigns of the Almighty God will provide comfort for our Causes, security in our beliefs, and assurance in our experiences BUT will never provide the contented peace that passes all understanding.

    A. If I worship the *"god of MY COMFORT"* I will live life inconsistently and will wander from Cause to Cause and force God to fit my agenda instead of crucifying Self and accepting God's commands (see Philippians 3:1-6).

    B. If I worship the *"god of MY SUCCESS"* I will limit the Almighty God to what I want Him to be and will never find the freedom that comes from knowing the whole Truth of God (see John 8:31-32).

    C. If I worship the *"god of MY NATION"* I will forever live enslaved to emotions or sensations and will never know the absolute security that is provided to those who follow Scripture (see 1 John 5:13).

II. The psychologizing of the modern mind has led us to reject the God of Scripture. Today's idolatry has changed our vocabulary. Now "sin" is "low self-esteem," "justification" is "experiencing God's affirmation," "sanctification" is accepting "self-worth," "salvation" is whatever the latest self-help fad offers. This redefining of God has led to abominations in our world (Deuteronomy 12:31).

There is one great tragedy that is evident—we may have lost a conscious awareness of sin and the vocabulary to identify sin, BUT we have not lost the guilt of sin or the need to have sin forgiven!

Modern man struggles to atone for this guilt but is helpless to find an answer because completely erased is the fact that Christ calls us to deny ourselves, take up our crosses, and daily follow Him in self-denial. Those who are caught in a profound self-absorption cannot understand this invitation because they are "joined to their idols!" Like ancient Israel (Hosea 4:17), such has been charmed to the extent he is joined together in an unquestioned league or union. He refuses to question his situation; he is fascinated. The Almighty God has become less appealing and, thus, easily replaced! Modern man has become totally charmed and has cast aside the one true Lord God Almighty for an image created to be a convenience for selfishness.

- 6 -

Restoring Reverence by Repentance

(Hebrews 12:28-29)

Introduction

I.   Idolatry is a foolish practice. Although its adherents may be sincere, they are wrong. They fashion a god that is comfortable to their lifestyles and vigorously support this idol. Without man's cunning, the idol would perish and man's folly would be exposed.

This truth is illustrated by the following: Fire symbolized the god of the Chaldeans. They carried their god into several countries proving that he was the greatest god. This god of fire challenged the images of gold, silver, brass, and wood and reduced them to ashes. By this contest the Chaldeans god was worshiped almost everywhere. But then he came to Egypt. The High Priest of Canopus thought of a strategy which would succeed in proving the Egyptian gods were superior to the Chaldeans. In Egyptian idolatry, purified water was used to purify the Nile water. The purification jars were cleverly constructed with small imperceptible holes. The High Priest took one of these jars and stopped the holes with wax and fitted the head of an idol in the jar's mouth. The Chaldeans challenged the Egyptian gods and the High Priest brought out the jar, filled with water. A fire was built and the jar set in its midst. The heat soon melted the wax; the water flowed out and extinguished the fire. Thus, Canopus was victorious over the Chaldeans!

II.   ⏎ Our series has forced us to admit that idolatry is not merely a practice of the ancients. ⏎ It is as prevalent today as it has ever been. ⏎ We have discovered a troubling fact—idolatry occurs with the redesigning of the biblical God into a god that fits OUR concepts and beliefs of how God should act.

⏎ The God of the Bible is not denied, just revised. God is welcomed as a gentle, permissive Friend—not as the sovereign, omnipotent Creator. ⏎ Consequently, religion has become a convenience for surplus time, a panacea for all troubles, and a license to demand the fulfillment of Self's desires.

⏎ Instead of a faith that brings us to our knees, we have created gods that neatly fit into our personal understanding, support our cause, give us the perfect experience, serve our comfort, assure individual success, and legitimize our national decay!

In no way does such an idolatrous faith bring us to the humility and reverence and awe expected by the biblical God!

III.   As we survey the current religious practices and observe the shocking absence of awe for the Almighty, we are perplexed.

Observe modern worshiping assemblies: ⏎ *"You may find much good, such a vibrant fellowship or inspirational teaching or emotional music, but too much of it happens on the horizontal plane, with only a courteous nod toward the vertical...The purpose of the whole enterprise, it seems, is to guarantee that everyone feel comfortable and entertained"* (McCullough, 110).

⏎ How can we recover what has been lost? How can we restore reverence?

The good news—the situation is not as hopeless as it appears! The awe that previously existed can be restored. ⏎ Two critical points will help us restore the reverence and awe for our Holy God:

A. A process of repentance which calls us back to reverence.

B. A guide which offers us infallible and authoritative instruction.

This lesson looks to the call of repentance that must be heeded before we can begin to follow anew the authoritative instruction given in His Word.

Body

There is only one way by which the lost awe and reverence can be restored—repentance! ⌖ To "repent" means to turn from one way (practice) and toward another (Acts 3:19; 2 Corinthians 7:10). ⌖ Biblical repentance is an on-going (constant) practice. As we mature in faith we come to understand sin better and we are expected to turn from this (1 John 1:6-10); we develop attitudes that are in conformity to God's Word (Romans 12:1-2; 2 Peter 1:5-11).

I.   The process of daily repentance is critical if we are to be kept from idolatry! Every day Satan tempts us to redesign the biblical God so our lives will be more comfortable and our beliefs more acceptable to the world. ⌖ There is a constant battle and we must practice daily repentance (2 Corinthians 10:5). ⌖ This is a great challenge—to let go of the god of our personal creation and restore reverence to the God of all creation! ⌖ This requires us to repent of self-centeredness!

The process of repentance that will restore our reverence has three steps:

A. ⌖ **REMEMBER!**

1. ⌖ The restoration of reverence begins where its loss started—with the memory of who God is, what He expects, and how we are to approach Him.

2. 2 Peter 3:1-2—There is a problem of "forgetfulness" which plagues Believers. John Bunyan's *Pilgrim's Progress* speaks of a certain place named "Forgetful Green." It is a most dreadful place for there the Christian pilgrim meets with great calamity—he forgets the great God. Many battles have been fought there and Satan was the victor because saints forgot the greatness of God!

3. ☝ When it comes to life we must not forget the greatness of the biblical God. *"We must pause long enough to become aware of our actual circumstances: our joyous gratitude, we discover, has led us into the throne room of the universe, and now we are in the presence of the Holy One who utterly transcends us, who holds together all creation from the smallest molecule to the largest galaxy and all history from the first page to the last, who is burning in wrath against sin with the flame of urging love, who has claimed us in Jesus Christ and will keep us in the embrace of grace for all eternity"* (McCullough, 111).

4. This remembrance of God should be intricately woven into the fabric of our daily events (Psalm 1:2; Genesis 39:9).

B. ☝ FOCUS!

1. ☝ Once we refuse to allow Satan to redefine the biblical God in our minds, we will keep a singular focus upon the Almighty as the One seated in heavenly splendor and ruling the Universe. This will cause us to lose sight of everything else. The commands of this Holy God will consume our attention.

2. ☝ This singular focus will be especially expressed in our worship.

The focus on worship is easily understandable. That which is worshipped in our hearts is our "god." The actions and expressions of our worship offer a tangible expression to the object of our worship. This is why there are "worship wars"—people who are zealous for the one true God are very zealous for His commanded worship. Those who demonstrate a casual shrug regarding the one true God will demonstrate a casual regard for the actions and expressions of worship to God. This is a clear consequential conclusion resulting from one's choice about the "god" in whom he believes.

For a clear illustration of how prevalent modern idolatry's insipid pollution has infected modern religion, look at the "worship" performed in modern churches.

If we seek to flee idolatry and follow the God of the Bible, all that we do in worship assemblies will be done to pay homage to this great God and express our willingness to serve Him throughout life.

3. 🖑 *"Sometimes what passes for worship is more human-centered than God-centered. We want to make sure everyone 'gets something' out of the experience and for good reason: this tends to be the standard most of us use to judge whether a service was 'meaningful' or not. Was I inspired? Were the sermon and music to MY liking? Were MY needs met? If not, well there' always another church down the street to try next Sunday...Much good results from the desire to be sensitive to the needs of the congregation, whether believers or seekers. But what difference does it make if God is not at the center?"* (McCullough, 113).

4. 🖑 The problem with many worship assemblies today is that the focus has changed. It is no longer focused upon the Lord God Almighty but upon man! Isaiah's complaint to ancient Israel is frighteningly illustrated in many worshipping assemblies today. Isaiah's response to a culture that had replaced the Almighty God with idols made in their own image was blunt, "You turn things upside down!" (Isaiah 29:16, ESV). Too many have forgotten that God Almighty is the focus. Worship is FOR God, not man.

Look carefully at this material that was taught in an adult Bible class on the topic of "worship"...

"We humans are capable of expressing worship toward God through a variety of emotional and physical responses" (Notes 1:2). **Note:** This does not say that some expressions are unauthorized and repulsive to God. All that is taught is a "freedom" to utilize any "physical" or "emotional" expression in worship.

augl

"Each of us will see God differently, and seek to worship Him differently...God has given to each of us a personality type that seeks to worship Him differently...Our God enjoys spontaneous, loving, heart-felt responses of any nature as long as they are authentic" (Notes 1:5-6). **Note:** This offers license to do anything as long as one deems it "authentic worship." There is stressed the legitimacy of each being "different" and being allowed to demonstrate that "difference" regardless of what God has commanded in worship. This contradicts the biblical teaching that Christians "all speak the same thing...be perfected together in the same mind" (1 Corinthians 1:10, ASV). This advice for each being allowed to express their differences openly and unrestricted is condemned by Inspiration. As the Church in Corinth devolved into confusion and chaos because its members believed this nonsense, God said such worshipping assemblies were reprehensible (1 Corinthians 11:17). This false teaching states that the only criteria for worship expressions are that one be "sincere."

"Our God has strange taste for He loves Rejoicing, Spontaneity, and Graciousness. He enjoys watching His children have fun and enjoy themselves...If He didn't specifically command it then it must not be important to Him and we should find freedom in permission to do the uncommanded" (Notes 1:12-13). **Note:** The emphasis of this false teaching is to provide the erring worshipper some foundation for actions and expressions that are *contrary* to what the Bible commands.

"1 Corinthians 14:26. Why is this not a part of our corporate worship when Scripture suggest that perhaps it should play a major part" (Notes 6:12). **Note:** This error encourages a repudiation of God's commanded actions and expressions of worship by saying the worship is to be directed to the worshippers rather than to God. And notice the cunning way in which biblical support is attempted by this phrase "Scripture suggest"—we do not look for "suggestions" because we look for "commands."

The real result of modern idolatry is seen in this comment—the focus is taken completely off God and placed onto the worshipper: *"Our services are to aid each worshipper to express in an individual personal fashion the thanksgiving and praise they need...all of us are unique and with special gifts by which we can best express ourselves"* (Notes 8:11). It is all "about ME" and God is pushed aside. Where is the biblical worship command for the congregation to come together as one cohesive Body and worship in one orderly expression so that the Almighty God is glorified? This comment simply calls for the glorification of each person's individualism!

It seems many are confused and think the worshipers are the audience, preachers are the entertainers, and God is the prompter. All is arranged and performed for the audience's applause.

Worship in this way is meaningful only if it strikes a responsive chord in those assembled ("Wow! That was a great worship—it really met MY needs!").

☝ It is easy to understand why God is redesigned...so He will sanction any kind of "wowing" worship practice. After all, if the focus of our worship is to elicit "Wows!" from the audience, then God must be a god of the "Holy wow!"

5. Repentance leads us to restore the focus of worship—it is FOR God, not man.

   a) ☝ Worship that is designed FOR man is idolatry (Exodus 20:3).
      to do things to make certain people happy

   b) ☝ Worship that unseats God as its primary focus is sin (2 Thessalonians 2:4; 2 Timothy 3:2).

   c) ☝ Worship that is focused upon pleasing man is blasphemy (Malachi 3:13-14).

6. ☝ We need to guard against redesigning God so that we fashion a god of worship that satisfies selfishness.

We are "at home" in worship ONLY when we focus solely upon God (Psalm 84:1-12; Zechariah 8:21).

C. ☞ **STRUCTURE!**

[handwritten: 1: Cor 14 } Study for 8-7]

1. ☞ Repentance leads us to focus upon God's greatness; and in order to focus properly we must have structure. God has revealed to us the structure of worship that He desires. ☞ Idolatry seeks to redesign this structure! (Consider how the situation described in 1 Corinthians 11:17 rebukes Christians who were coming together for a "Christian worship assembly"— there were no graven images of Baal or Moloch, but it was still idolatry!).

2. In creating man, God knew that there would be a need for certain rituals and patterns that would give man the means for worship.

   ☞ Worship cannot be left to the whimsical nature of man. ☞ Worship cannot become man's self-expression of his various talents. This is why God has COMMANDED the actions and expressions of acceptable worship!

   This biblical conclusion is blatantly ignored in false teaching:

   "What makes worship beautiful is that it comes from the heart's outpouring, and when authentic, God is pleased...The worshipper determines when JOY (celebrating; laughter; clapping; shouts from the audience; etc.) rather than AWE is appropriate...David's response came from the heart. He did what his heart told him to do and it was acceptable to God as worship because it was authentic!" (Notes 1:9). This statement of false teaching emphasizes the sin of idolatry—Self decides what is appropriate and not God's revealed commands!

   Those seeking to practice modern idolatry worship a god of their own imaginations. They seek to offer biblical support by advocating a permissive silence of the Bible—*"If the Bible is silent on what we want to do then we are free to do it!"* Note this comment: *"Where Scripture is silent, certainly someone has to decide what is expedient—that ought to be left to the* _decision makers who are having to ask, 'What is needed NOW?'"_ (Notes 7:11).

Idolatry worships "comfort" and uses that to manipulate others to accept actions and expressions of worship that God has not commanded. Attempting to manipulate by guilt those who object to idolatrous actions and expressions in worship is this comment: _"If I am uncomfortable with some change does that mean God is uncomfortable?"_ (Notes 7:13). The suggestion is that anyone who objects to being "uncomfortable" with changes, actions or expressions in worship that are unbiblical, should not say a word—it is not their position to say they are "uncomfortable!" And yet the idolater will freely whine about being made to feel "uncomfortable" by the biblical traditions that have long been practiced (2 Thessalonians 2:15).

A very important question to ask the modern idolater, "Who are you more concerned about being uncomfortable—yourself or God?"

God Almighty is uncomfortable when His commands are not followed (Psalm 7:11; 11:7; Malachi 1:7-14; 2:17; Revelation 2:12; 2:20; 3:16).

Faithful Christians are uncomfortable when they are confronted by those who do not follow God's commands (Ezekiel 2:1-8; Jeremiah 9:2, 3; 2 Corinthians 6:14-16; Ephesians 5:3-11).

Individualism often corrupts biblical worship and invites idolatry. Those seeking to advance false teaching regarding God stress this individualism. _"God wired all of us differently...BE OURSELVES—to worship God in our own unique and different way. We can then use the gifts and special wiring that God placed in each of us"_ (Notes 7:14). Here is the foundation of modern idolatry: each is permitted to do as he chooses; there are no definite commanded actions or expressions; and all is permitted, nothing is wrong. If you want "authority," idolatry says to simply ask one of the leaders in the congregation to give you permission.

The great God of the Bible has given us a pattern by which He is to be praised (John 4:24).

3. ⌖ Our idolatrous culture redesigns God's patterns. It scoffs at traditions, rituals, and patterns.

"A Jewish Rabbi (Abraham Joshua Heschel) was once confronted with a complaint about the worship in his congregation. Some told him the worship did not express what they wanted to feel and asked him to change it. Heschel told them that the worship was not to give them the feelings they wanted but it was for them to learn to sense what the worship taught (honor to God)" (McCullough, 115).

4. The biblical God has expressly commanded and justly expects man to follow the structure of worship that will keep our hearts focused upon Him. ⌖ Only those who seek to idolize ungodly actions and expressions will redesign a god who will accept less than what the biblical God has commanded!

II. ⌖ There is a biblical illustration that fits well in this lesson (Exodus 19:10-14).

When God reveals Himself, man has no choice but to prepare himself to meet this majestic God. This preparation will help us to restore the reverence that our great God deserves. Notice what is involved:

A. Prepare with the realization that the **LORD** God Almighty is present (Exodus 19:10).

The title **LORD** is most significant. It is a title that identifies the Holy God Almighty—no other is equal. No triviality is acceptable (Exodus 20:18-23). It is time for the most somber and reverent actions and expressions of worship. It is a summons to be in the presence of the Almighty.

B. ⌖ Prepare with consecration (Exodus 19:10).

This requires us to separate from sin and demonstrate pure dedication to God. You cannot give reverence to the true God if you have not spurned sin. The one true God can never be revered by one whose life harbors sin (2 Corinthians 6:17; Psalm 59:2).

C. ⌐ Prepare with willing obedience (Exodus 19:10bff).

Some of the commands seem trivial but they are required by God. We are obligated to do everything God says; do not trivialize any command! Those who demonstrate reverence humbly obey every command. Verse 12 leaves no room for changing God's commands, "You shall set bounds for the people."

D. ⌐ Prepare with the appointed time (Exodus 19:11).

God had given a set time and that time was to be restricted for God. Thus, reverence is found by those who prepare for the appointed times of worship. Reverence is demonstrated by the schedules and priorities of everyday living.

Conclusion

I. ⌐ Reverence can be restored! Those who repent, refocus, and follow God's structure find that the lost reverence is restored (Isaiah 57:17-19; Psalm 51:12).

II. ⌐ There is a great desire to restore reverence by using this three-step process. But...

1. How are we to know true repentance?

2. How are we to know which focus is the right one?

3. How are we to know the right structure?

The answers to these important questions cannot be found in rituals or culture. There is an infallible source that gives us assurance that our following the three steps to restoration is right—the Word of God! God's Word is more important than any other instruction. We look next at how this Word can lead us confidently to a restoration of reverence for the Almighty God!

III.   A little boy was asked, "How many gods are there?" He quickly replied, "Only one!" "How do you know this?" "Because there is room for only One. God fills the heaven and earth."

Let us find comfort in this simple understanding.

🖱 There is but ONE true God. Let all cast away the gods of their imaginations. 🖱 Let us turn to the one, true God and submit to His directions in our life. 🖱 You may not like what the God of the Bible teaches, commands, and condemns, but do you really have another option? No. 🖱 There is but ONE true God!

- 7 -

Restoring Reverence with Authority

(Hebrews 12:28-29)

Introduction

I. 🖰 We live in times...

A. Where God is respected but not revered.

B. Where people trust in the supernatural but not the supernatural God of Scriptures.

C. Where feelings outweigh faith; hope has been usurped by hopelessness.

D. Where religious devotion is practiced more like a picnic than the knee-knocking, heart-pricking experience of Scripture.

II. Indications of our lost reverence are all around us.

A. 🖰 **Biblical reverence honors God with dress.**

In Scripture those who approached God in worship wore the best garments (Exodus 28:2, 43). Past generations owned "Sunday-go-to-meeting" clothes.

aug 15

These may have been overalls, but they were the best garments owned and use was restricted to church going!

It was common to hear mothers instruct their children, "You go change. We're going to worship and you know better than to wear that! God deserves your best. Wear your best for the Lord!"

This practical code of dress existed because of reverent respect for the Lord God Almighty. The loss of reverence is indicated today by the lax dress that many wear to worship. Obviously a consideration of modesty is needed in determining what to wear (i.e. just because you have a tux in your closet does not mean you have to wear that to every church worship assembly). Some may not even have "dress clothes" to wear to services. However, many that do have nicer clothes choose not to wear them and wear things that show they have a trivial view toward the dedicated worship service to the Lord. Many dress better for a school/business/funeral function than they do for assemblies where the Lord God Almighty is worshiped! Reverence in worship is not shown by dress that is appropriate for a picnic.

B. Biblical reverence honors God with speech.

In Scripture those who approached God in prayer, singing, or preaching did so with awe. They addressed the Almighty in terms of respect and fear. The loss of reverence today is seen in prayers offered to "Daddy," in songs designed to make worshipers giddy, and in preaching that has forgotten the term "sin" and seldom calls for self-denial.

C. Biblical reverence honors God with first fruits.

In Scripture those who revered God recognized God's ownership of possessions. They never allowed Self to receive better than God!

Today the loss of reverence appears as many feed Self their first fruits and offer God their leftovers.

The priority of giving to the Church is replaced by the priority of giving to Self. We cannot give God the first-fruits of our money because we have allowed Self to spend us into debt; we cannot give God the first-fruits of our time because we have allowed Self to convince us that there are other *more important* things that take us away from worship or Bible study!

D. How did we lose the reverence? The answer is simple but disturbing. In fact, some angrily deny the answer; they stubbornly refuse to look at the facts.

The answer—🖰 **IDOLATRY!**

Modern man has taken the biblical God and redesigned Him to fit today's culture. This revamped "god" is used to sanction the idolatry of causes, biblical ignorance, experiences, comfort, success, and national sins.

The subtlety of this is frightening—few recognize it; fewer confess it! Such is sinful because Self is in control (Colossians 3:5b).

🖰 How disturbing is it to hear that modern worshipers approach the Almighty with a "casual nod" or a "yawn of familiarity?" Such should stir within each a zeal to correct this failing (Acts 17:23b; Psalms 135:5; 33:22; 40:22-23; Jeremiah 10:10).

🖰 The failure to offer correction and the willingness to accept the redesigned "god" causes us to ask troubling questions. 🖰 "Why are we silent? Why do we allow the biblical God to be redesigned? Have we lost the reverence and awe for the biblical God?" (Ezekiel 33:7).

III. The road to recovery of reverence is mapped by two points (Ezekiel 14:6):

A. 🖰 **A process of repentance**—we must turn away from idolatry and return to biblical awe. This is accomplished by:

1. Remembering the majesty of God (Isaiah 40:22-23).

2. Focusing upon God-centered worship and living (2 Timothy 3:4b; Malachi 3:13-18).

3. Structuring our worship and lives according to God's directions (1 Corinthians 4:6; 15:58).

B. ✧ **A guide offering infallible instructions**—we must follow the commands of God if we are to revere God (John 4:24; Deuteronomy 12:31-32).

Body

I. Critical to the process of repentance is the standard by which repentance is commanded. One may turn from one idol but turn to another idol unless he has the right directions (1 Kings 20:23; 2 Kings 17:33-34; 18:4).

Thus, there must be a standard by which one can turn from idols and toward the Almighty (1 Thessalonians 1:9b).

Ezekiel 18:30-32—There is a definite standard that judges conduct (verse 30a); requires a turning (verse 30b); identifies certain things as wrong (verse 30c); leads to newness (verse 31); and condemns, if ignored (verse 32).

II. As critical as the process of repentance is to restoring the lost reverence, there is something MORE critical—that which directs our religious actions!

A. ✧ The infallible guide for restoring the lost reverence is the Word of God (Scripture).

Our modern age has experienced an explosion of words. We are bombarded with so many words, from so many places and by so many methods that words have lost their significance.

Words today have lost the sense of absolute—they are plastic and can be molded to fit any individual's purpose. There is lacking any sense of universal meaning. So we are told today, "There is no language of truth." Those who accept a plastic vocabulary are prime targets for idolatry because a "god" can be redefined, revamped, and redesigned with a few plastic words.

Any sense of absolute authority in religious faith is denied. Mankind is left without certainty in faith, confounded in practice, and miserable in idolatry!

The answer to the modern muddle of meaningless words is the Word of God (1 Corinthians 1:25; Hebrews 4:12):

1. Here are words that could never come from the idols of man's design.

2. Here are words with absolute meaning and specific application.

B. How can we hear God's Word today? It is common to hear people say, "God led me to this..." Is this how God's directions are made known?

How can we distinguish between what God actually says and what our selfish desires wish?

We are told to test religious instructions (1 John 4:1). Thankfully, God has provided an absolute way by which His Word can be known—the Bible! All desires, feelings, intuitions, dreams, inner voices, etc., must be evaluated by this Word.

How do we "hear" God's Word today? There are three primary ways:

1. The **WRITTEN Word—the Scriptures.**

The Bible is God's Word that tells us exactly what God desires. A written Word is the best method of communicating God's will; and it alone is capable of directing us in repentance from the idols we desire. When people follow God's Word, they turn from idolatry (1 Thessalonians 1:9; 2:13). However there is a problem. People will not read the Bible! It is available. It is clearly translated. It is recognized as the Word of God. But people will not read it!

The Bible teaches that one who reveres God will cherish and read the revealed Word (Psalm 119:18, 24, 28, 31).

The problem with modern idolaters is that they do not have a devoted heart to read and study the Word of God (Psalm 119:36, 47). Today many profess to believe in the Bible as the Word of God, but their profession is betrayed as a lie because they do not read or study it.

For many the only time that any spiritual nourishment is obtained is when attending Bible classes or listening to sermons. One has described such type of nourishment at that time as a baby bird with a wide mouth where anything can be stuffed inside!

To many Christians, Bible study and Bible reading is drudgery. BUT they can spend hours on Facebook or some other form of social media. Why can they spend so much time on Facebook and not find it boring; but they cannot find even a miniscule of time, interest and commitment to read the Bible? Why must congregations be prodded to be daily Bible readers, and even with the urging only a small percentage will read their Bible on a daily schedule? With an understanding of this unwillingness of Christians to be daily Bible readers, there should be no surprise at the rampant idolatry that is based upon individualism!

The truism states, "We are what we read." The basic truth of that truism is that upon whatever object our focus is set, that is what we will become. Those whose focus is on God's Word will practice a devout reading and study and they will be "transformed" by that Word (Hebrews 12:1, 2). Those whose focus is a devout reading other than God's Word will be transformed by that material as well. As Hosea lamented, "They became as detestable as that which they loved" (Hosea 9:10). There is nothing wrong with a wide scope of reading, but there is a problem when the reading and studying of God's Holy Scriptures becomes less important than time on Facebook, Twitter, Snap Chat, or other literary materials. How can one profess to believe the Bible is God's Holy Word but NOT read it on a devout schedule???

 Biblical illiteracy allows idolatry. Such happened to Israel (Psalm 97:7) and it will happen to Christians (2 Timothy 2:15). Why has biblical illiteracy grown to such amazing proportions?

a. *"Bible studies have given way to support groups and classes on 'practical' topics, such as parenting or coping with stress. Even pastors [sic] shy away from conferences offering serious biblical/theological reflection in favor of learning the latest techniques for church growth"* (McCullough, 123).

b. Another reason is found in the impact of idolatry. People look at the Bible as something to be studied in Bible class but not as the rule for life.

One politician explained his immoral behavior with his "religious practices" as stating he is able to "compartmentalize" various aspects of his life so each aspect is distinct and not influenced by the other aspects. So he was very comfortable and content to profess a strong religious practice and also be involved in immorality. He said that he could "leave" the things pertaining to God in the Church building and then leave the "other things" outside of religion. His explanation reflects the basic attitudes of modern Americans.

People can thus accept the Bible, redesign God to fit their individual tastes, and live contrary to everything the Bible teaches! When they see something in Scripture that is uncomfortable or that does not fit "their" Christianity, they quickly dismiss it or try to rediscover the real meaning of the passage so that the new meaning exonerates them of any guilt.

c. Many are unwilling to study the Scriptures to understand what it teaches. Most are willing to study it with a neutral, all-permissive approach that bows down to their "god of understanding." To these the "god of personal experience" is much more comfortable than the Jehovah of Scripture.

Too many are willing to talk "about" the Bible but never talk "from" the Bible; generalizations, not specifics, are cherished because generalizations can be as plastic as our modern vocabulary!

d. When the Word of God is present it rebukes idolatry. We MUST restore reverence by knowing the written Word! (1 Kings 22:9-23).

e. 1 Kings 13 is a text that teaches a failure to discern what Truth is and that a religious lie leads to destruction. Many today are ignorant of the Bible and so they accept as authority man's word.

Those seeking to practice modern idolatry worship a god of their own imaginations. They seek to offer biblical support by advocating a permissive silence of the Bible—*"If the Bible is silent on what we want to do then we are free to do it!"* Note this comment: *"Where Scripture is silent, certainly someone has to decide what is expedient—that ought to be left to the decision makers who are having to ask, 'What is needed NOW?'"* (Notes 7:11).

Individualism corrupts biblical worship and invites idolatry. Those seeking to advance false teaching regarding God stress this individualism. *"God wired all of us differently...BE OURSELVES—to worship God in our own unique and different way. We can then use the gifts and special wiring that God placed in each of us"* (Notes 7:14). **Notice:** Here is the foundation of modern idolatry. Each is permitted to do as he chooses. No definite commanded actions or expressions, all is permitted; nothing is wrong. If you want "authority" then simply ask one of the "Leaders" in the congregation who will give you permission.

2. The PROCLAIMED Word—The Teachings.

The absolute Word of God is proclaimed in many ways: ✑ private teaching, classrooms, the pulpit. ✑There ought to be a reverent awe that accompanies any proclamation of God's Word. "Thus saith the Lord" identifies the proclamation as deserving special honor. How tragic that some do not reverence God's Word in this way (2 Peter 3:16b).

Biblical proclamation involves much more than sharing experiences or talking in generalities.

"It is as itself the Word, the power sharper than any two-edge sword, the power of the universe-creating, history-making, truth-telling, sin-annulling, death-defeating, life-giving, grace-granting, Kingdom-bringing Word" (McCullough, 125).

✑ Biblical proclamation is the speaking of God's Word! Modern culture has redesigned this. Huck Finn commented on the preacher-farmer, Mr. Phelps, that he "never charged nothing for his preaching. And it was worth it too."

The Word proclaimed is a powerful force (Romans 1:16; 1 Thessalonians 2:13), but it faces the opposition of our idolatrous culture. ✑ Today's idolatry is not satisfied with the simple gospel (1 Corinthians 1:18-29).

As you proclaim the Gospel, are you reverent?

✑ *"May God deliver us from preachers insensible of the dangers. Those who are full of beans and confident in their gifts, who project an image of smooth certainty and easy familiarity with the Almighty, who demonstrate no agony of spirit or terror before the holy, had best start doing something more useful...for the sort of god they preach is a god too trivial to take seriously"* (McCullough, 128).

The only way for true repentance, that repentance which will restore the lost reverence, to be known is for the Word to be proclaimed.

This will not lead one to win popularity; it will bring confrontations; it will even cause one to doubt and question absolute Truth, but it must be done (2 Timothy 4:2-5)!

Beware! Idolatry seeks to persuade you to redesign the proclamation so that it is less than (or more than) what God commands.

3. The PRACTICED Word—The Obedience.

As one encounters God's Word, there will be change.

 That which is read, understood, and believed, becomes practiced. The power of the Word invades every part of our being and changes our lives (Ephesians 5:1-21). No longer will the individual idols be our cherished gods. They will be cast out as repentance turns us back to the Holy God.

- We will once again crucify self.

- We will refuse to twist the Scriptures.

- We will admit God's sovereignty over all.

- We will experience reverence and awe.

- We will worship in joy, knowing that we are doing what the Holy God has commanded and we are honoring His wishes not entertaining our wants.

C. There is a biblical illustration that fits this lesson (Exodus 19:8).

For 400 years Israel had been exposed to idolatry. The evil had invaded her religious practices. Now she had reached Mt. Sinai and was faced with a sobering fact—there is no god except Jehovah God!

Israel's understanding led her to reject all gods except for Jehovah. This response illustrates that which ought to be seen as God's Word brings repentance:

1. *It was prompt!* They did not hesitate.

2. *It was sincere!* They had no reservations.

3. *It was unanimous!* All together—no individualistic tastes!

4. Israel thus responded because she had no other option. She stood face-to-face with the Sovereign Lord God.

   a. How could she redesign Him?

   b. How could she revamp His character?

   c. How could she rewrite His commands?

   ✍ She was uncomfortable before this God, but she dared not change Him. Such modifications were intolerable (Exodus 20:22-23). You would think Israel would forever recall this event but she promised more than she was willing to perform.

Conclusion

I.   ✍ Exodus 19:17a—Moses brought Israel out to "meet" God. The root word for the term translated "meet" *"denotes a planned encounter wherein the subject intentionally confronts the object...can represent friendly encounters...or going out to meet someone in order to recognize or gain him as an ally...Such meetings are purposeful and intentional"* (Harris, 811).

Moses knew Israel must reverence the Almighty God and she must reject her idols. He brought her information and urged upon her the action that was necessary. She then decided to reverence and awe God.

II.   Each of us stands where Moses stood. We know there is no other god except Jehovah God.

A. Has our reverence and awe of The Almighty been compromised?

B. Have we redesigned God?

C. Have we modified God's commands so they are more "comfortable"?

D. Have we lessened our proclamation of God's Word and softened the absolutes of God's Truth? When you bring people to "meet" God, what kind of God do they meet?

- 8 -

Guarding the Reverence (Pt. 1)

(Exodus 32:1-5)

Introduction

I.   🖐 The greatest danger we face and the most lethal and cunning evil Satan utilizes is 🖐 "apathy." The insidious evil is subtle and seldom realized until it is too late. Apathy has led to the devastation of civilizations. The Lord's Church is not immune to apathy. The Lord's Church is often the unsuspecting victim as congregational members are content to drift along resting in a false assurance that things are going well. The majority of the members are unaware of the unrest and troubles threatening the congregation's fidelity to God's commands. Leaders who are apathetic are the weakest points because they are susceptible to Satan's suggestions on change. History provides a number of illustrations of how apathy has brought devastation.

A.   One of the most notable historical references on apathy comes from the throes of Hitler's death camp. In 1934, Martin Niemöller started the Pastors' Emergency League to defend the church. Hitler became angered by Niemöller's rebellious sermons and popularity and had him arrested on July 1, 1937. He was tried the following year and sentenced to seven months in prison and fined. He found himself suffering the fate that millions of others had suffered as he remained silent. In retrospect he recalled his silence when others were arrested and he penned these historic words: "First they came for the Communists, and I didn't speak up, because I wasn't a Communist. Then they came for the Jews, and I didn't speak up, because I wasn't a Jew. Then they came for the Catholics, and I didn't speak up, because I was a Protestant. Then they came for me, and by that time there was no one left to speak up for me" (Martin Niemöller in 1946). This comment was an indictment that those in Germany had been complicit by their silence when the Nazi regime imprisoned, persecuted, and murdered millions of people.

Niemöller's comment highlights the subtle and savage consequences that arise when people allow apathy to corrupt the national awareness.

B. Perhaps the most notable historic reference on spiritual apathy is found in the prophet's words as he surveyed the smoldering ruins of Jerusalem and the conquered citizens marching into exile.

"How lonely sits the city that was full of people! She has become like a widow who was *once* great among the nations! She who was a princess among the provinces has become a forced laborer!...'Is it nothing to all you who pass this way? Look and see if there is any pain like my pain which was severely dealt out to me, which the LORD inflicted on the day of His fierce anger'" (Lamentations 1:1, 12).

Jeremiah's prophecy is filled with charges of how Judah's leaders (government and religious) were complicit in the fall of the nation. These had heard God's Truth proclaimed but they had chosen to ignore it. Apathy controlled their choices.

C. The insidious evil of apathy would be utilized by Satan to attack and destroy the People of God in the New Testament. This attack plan is summarized by Paul's exhortation to the elders of the Ephesian Church of Christ.

"You yourselves know, from the first day that I set foot in Asia, how I was with you the whole time, serving the Lord with all humility and with tears and with trials which came upon me through the plots of the Jews; how I did not shrink from declaring to you anything that was profitable, and teaching you publicly and from house to house, solemnly testifying to both Jews and Greeks of repentance toward God and faith in our Lord Jesus Christ...For I did not shrink from declaring to you the whole purpose of God. Be on guard for yourselves and for all the flock, among which the Holy Spirit has made you overseers, to shepherd the church of God which He purchased with His own blood. I know that after my departure savage wolves will come in among you, not sparing the flock; and from among your own selves men will arise, speaking perverse things, to draw away the disciples after them. Therefore be on the alert, remembering that night and day for a period of three years I did not cease to admonish each one with tears. And now I commend you to God and to the word of His grace, which is able to build you up and to give you the inheritance among all those who are sanctified. I have coveted no one's silver or gold or clothes" (Acts 20:18-33).

Paul did all he could to urge the elders to be on guard against the evil of apathy that would lead the Church away from fidelity to God's commands.

1. He had shown them his personal example of zealousness in holding fast God's commands—"did not shrink" (no cowering; boldness).

2. He had shown them the absolute governing that was to be used by the congregation—the "whole" counsel of God (all of God's instructions and commands).

3. He urged the elders to be "on guard/alert"—be vigilant; refuse to be apathetic. The term "guard/alert/watch" is from the Greek term *Γρηγορεύω* (grēgoreuō gray-gor-yoo'-o) which refers to a sentry's duty to *keep awake*, to *watch*, be vigilant, wake, be watchful. The term describes the obligation of a sentry who is entrusted with the safety and security of others. There is trust and confidence placed in this sentry that he will perform his

79

duty with fidelity. Such a metaphor well describes the duty that has been accepted by the elders who are the "sentries" of the Lord's Church.

4. He warned that Satan would attack God's Church and that the attack would come from "within" the eldership itself!

5. He warned that the Church would be encouraged to follow "perverse things." The word translated as "perverse" is significant in describing the devilish strategy of those seeking to change God's commands and lead the Church into apostasy.

The word "perverse" is from the Greek διαστρέφω (diastrephō dee-as-tref'-o) and means to *distort*, to *misinterpret*, to *corrupt* so that what was truth is redefined and has become polluted so that it leads one to turn away from the original.

II.	Modern idolatry exists today and is permitted to do its insidious evil because of apathy. There is no one who is "on guard." This has resulted because of the following influences.

A. The culture of "tolerance" has eliminated the biblical God of exclusiveness.

B. The culture of "individualism" has trumped the self-sacrificing, cross-bearing discipleship required in New Testament Christianity. No longer is there the knee knocking fear that one has offended the Lord God Almighty. No longer is sincere repentance demanded. What we witness is a replication of the situation at Belshazzar's Feast in Daniel 5:6. Except the callous hearts today do not even demonstrate the reverent dread that the pagan Emperor did!

C. The culture of "spiritual anarchy" has erased the governing authority of the inspired Bible. Spiritual anarchy has arisen because of the dearth of biblical knowledge. People are ignorant about what the Scriptures teach! The only time any effort is made to "study" the Bible is when one happens to attend a Bible class or listen to a sermon. They are willing to be fed like little birds with their mouths open and anything is stuffed into them! There is no discernment because there is no knowledge of God's Word!

1. Those who fail to study, learn and discern spiritual Truth are controlled by their ignorance and stumble as they go forward. "The way of the wicked is like darkness; they do not know over what they stumble" (Proverbs 4:19).

2. Knowing God's Truth protects us. But modern idolatry causes us to turn away from Bible Truth and follow our own understanding. This results in disastrous consequences. "Guard your steps as you go to the house of God and draw near to listen rather than to offer the sacrifice of fools; for they do not know they are doing evil" (Ecclesiastes 5:1).

3. How damning are the actions of those who decide they know better than God Almighty and they can improve on God's Church and modify the Almighty's character! "An ox knows its owner, and a donkey its master's manger, But Israel does not know, my people do not understand." (Isaiah 1:3; See also Isaiah 59:8).

   It is heartbreaking for the Almighty to make this comment about those who should be steadfast and loyal to the divine commands. But they have chosen to redesign God and rethink the divine commands: "They do not know, nor do they understand" (Isaiah 44:18). This reveals a willing rejection; a stubborn arrogance.

   The tragedy waiting for those demonstrating this callous arrogance is pronounced: "But evil will come on you which you will not know how to charm away; and disaster will fall on you for which you cannot atone; and destruction about which you do not know will come on you suddenly" (Isaiah 47:11).

4. Why are elders allowing the congregation (over which they have been appointed by the Holy Spirit to "shepherd") to suffer this famine of God's Word? Why are elders allowing spiritual anarchy to exist where every man does whatever "he" thinks is right and he is allowed the "right" to make

changes that he deems are needed for the congregation? The damnable condition of ancient Judah's spiritual ignorance is reflected in today's modern congregations!

🖱 "For My people are foolish, they know Me not; they are stupid children and have no understanding. They are shrewd to do evil, but to do good they do not know" (Jeremiah 4:22; See also Jeremiah 5:4). Look closely at each of these damnable points. One alone is tragic, but when combined they describe a situation that is unbelievable. This is the way the Almighty Good views those who seek to redesign the Holy God into a "more meaningful" entity that is "more comfortable" and communicates "more readily" to the modern mind! How could a congregation of God's people allow themselves to devolve to such a blasphemous condition? The answer is simple—they refused to ready, study, and apply God's Truth. They did just the opposite of Ezra (Ezra 7:10).

a) *They are* "foolish"—This is a term that is from a root term meaning to be *perverse* or *silly*. It can also be translated to refer to something "thick," and in this instance would refer to a "thick-brained man" (one incapable of learning). Such a person is lacking sense and generally corrupt. *"It is a term that primarily refers to moral perversion or insolence; to what is sinful rather than to mental stupidity. Such a person is a scoffer at Truth and is insolent, impatient with discipline and despises wisdom. He chooses based upon selfishness and rejects God's Truth. A fool feels his own way is without error thus does not listen to counsel of those older and wiser* (Harris, 19).

b) *They "know Me not"*—This refers to a variety of senses that are utilized in knowing another person. *"It refers to knowing through observation and a recognition of impact in one's life. It refers to having an acquaintance and awareness; a familiar friend; kinsfolk; have respect.*

The closest synonyms are "to discern" and "to recognize." It is used to describe the most personal acquaintances as when God "knows" Moses by name and face to face (Exodus 33:17; Deuteronomy 34:10).

This term is also used to describe man's relationship with other gods (idols) as in Deuteronomy 13:3, 7, 14 or with Jehovah God Almighty (1 Samuel 2:12; 3:7). The heathen do not "know" God (Jeremiah 10:25) and neither does Israel or anyone who redesigns God (Jeremiah 4:22)" (Harris, 366).

c) *"They are "stupid"*—*This term usually expresses one's lack of moral or spiritual understanding because of a willful rejection. Thus Saul acted as a "fool" when he offered the sacrifice (1 Samuel 13:13). He acted foolishly rather than from wisdom and confidence in following God's commands. This practical atheism was described by the Babylonians as "living in a ramanishu," i.e. living by one's own resources without dependence upon God. Such is the essence of idolatry!*

"This term refers to more than a lack of understanding. It refers to a deliberate rejection and spiritual apostasy. Such are wise to do evil but devoid of the knowledge to do good (Jeremiah 4:22)" (Harris, 624).

d) *They have "no understanding"*—This term refers to one's unwillingness to *understand*—to attend, consider, be diligent, discern, inform, instruct, have intelligence, be prudent, (deal) wisely.

"The verb refers to knowledge that is superior to facts—*one may have facts but not know how to use them. Thus it is necessary to know (understand) how to use the knowledge. It refers to perception (Psalm 73:22). Thus those who redesign God and refashion God's worship and commands have "no understanding"*—*they are lacking proper judgment and perceptive insight. They think they "know" God but they do not "understand" God"* (Harris, 103-104).

e) *They are "shrewd to do evil"*—The term "wise" denotes intelligence that brings success. This "wisdom" is urged by Proverbs in a positive manner—through it one will find God and success. *"The term refers to a manner of thinking and attitude regarding life. Sadly, Jeremiah observes that those devoted to redesigning God are utilizing 'wisdom' to pursue evil. They are cunning and crafty in their actions and seek to do the very opposite of God's righteous commands"* (Harris, 282).

f) *"To do good they know not"*—This term refers to the spiritual bankruptcy of those seeking to redesign God. They profess they know him but they are "worthless" (Titus 1:16). These are reprobates! This summarizes the end result of those who seek to change God's commands—in the end they have brought ruin and blasphemy even though they claimed to seek the opposite results.

☝ The saddest irony of idolatry—☝ those involved in *redesigning* God and *rethinking* God's commands and *refashioning* God's worship think they are pleasing God but they are breaking His heart, stirring His wrath and leading themselves and others to Hell!

They casually assert, *"Each of us will see God differently, and seek to worship Him differently...Our God has strange taste for He loves Rejoicing, Spontaneity, and Graciousness. He enjoys watching His children have fun and enjoy themselves...If He didn't specifically command it then it must not be important to Him and we should find freedom in permission to do the uncommanded"* (Notes 1:5, 3:12).

Those seeking to make worship more "exhilarating" and "meaningful" are consumed by a cancerous selfishness that has excluded God as it sought to serve Self's interests!

"Again we recall this statement from a previous class: A Jewish Rabbi (Abraham Joshua Heschel) was once confronted with a complaint about the worship in his congregation. Some told him the worship did not

express what they wanted to feel and asked him to change it. Heschel told them that the worship was not to give them the feelings they wanted but it was for them to learn to sense what the worship taught (honor to God) (McCullough, 115).

How dare anyone think himself to be more knowledgeable that the Almighty God and thus capable of redesigning God's revealed will to mankind! (Jeremiah 8:7).

Listen to the Almighty's attitude toward those who think they can blithely *redesign* God's character, *dismiss* God's commands, and *restructure* God's worship...

"Woe to them, for they have strayed from Me! Destruction is theirs, for they have rebelled against Me! ...they speak lies against Me. And they do not cry to Me from their heart when they wail on their beds...They turn away from Me. Although I trained and strengthened their arms, yet they devise evil against Me...Their princes will fall because of the insolence of their tongue" (Hosea 7:13-16).

D. There has been a dramatic tectonic shift in the world's religious conditions that has destroyed the foundations of faith and practice. This has resulted in the biblical God being redesigned in forms that contradict clear biblical texts. Especially is this evident in the American religious landscape.

E. The deconstruction of biblical Christianity has resulted in a reprehensible and blasphemous idolatry in worship actions and expressions.

Those responsible see no damage as a result of their actions. The "Change Agents" boastfully strut thinking their damnable actions and teachings are heroic. The "shepherds" of God's People have silently sat and complacently allowed the reverence for the Almighty to be polluted and their flock, over which the Holy Spirit has placed them, has been devoured. The members have sat compliantly and blindly followed the piping of irreligion without thought or objection as they were led into an abysmal irreverence.

III. In this lesson we return to the gold calf idolatry event at Sinai (Exodus 32) and discover directions for modern man on how he must react to modern idolatry. Only this behavior will be pleasing to God and only this action will confront the evil of modern idolatry's redesign of God's character and doctrine.

Body

I. ☝ God's expectations of His People when idolatry is present.

What do you do when you witness people redesigning God's commands so the commands are "more exhilarating" and "more meaningful"? Do you sit mumbling your objections in whispered tones? No! That is not the response God expects His dedicated People to demonstrate. Passivity, compromise, and timidity are NOT what the Almighty God expects from those who sincerely seek Him.

From the golden calf event we discover twelve points that offer instruction on how we must deal with idolatry. These twelve points highlight responses God expects to be seen in His Church as modern idolaters seek to modify and change the revealed commands and patterns.

A. **Courage not cowering**—"Aaron said to them, 'Tear off the gold rings which are in the ears of your wives, your sons, and your daughters, and bring them to me.' Then all the people tore off the gold rings which were in their ears and brought them to Aaron" (Exodus 32:2, 3). "Then Moses said to Aaron, What did this people do to you, that you have brought such great sin upon them?" (32:21).

   1. Aaron was held accountable for the idolatry that erupted in Israel's camp. He was in charge. He had the authority. The people recognized Aaron's authority because they went to him to ask for the idol. He could have stopped it. But he did not.

2. Conflict is unavoidable. Conflict will arise in the Lord's Church. God's Word gives us strict instructions about how we are to respond to conflict—face it; confront it; use the Inspired Word to resolve it (2 Timothy 1:7).

3. At one congregation in west Tennessee an Elder told me, "We want everyone to be happy. We don't want to lose anyone." The comment was made because there was a group in the congregation seeking to undermine the eldership and initiate "changes" that would "improve" the congregation. The eldership did not want such changes to occur in the congregation and were opposed to such changes but they acted as Aaron and tried to avoid conflict. But it did not work. A courageous response would have saved that congregation much turmoil.

4. When modern idolatry rears its blasphemous attitudes in a congregation, it is time for elders and members to stand firm and be uncompromising. They will be ridiculed, mocked, criticized and slandered. They will be called "ungodly traditionalists" and their spiritual maturity and knowledge of God's Word will be impugned. But they MUST stand firm in their allegiance to the Almighty God. When you are holding to the Truth, do not be intimidated to relent in your commitment or question the integrity of God's Word (Titus 1:9).

B. **Education in Truth not enabling error from ignorance**—"This is your god, O Israel, who brought you up from the land of Egypt" (32:4). "They have made for themselves a molten calf, and have worshiped it and have sacrificed to it and said, 'This is your god'" (32:8).

1. Ancient Israel had just witnessed the omnipotence of God Almighty (Exodus 19:16). They failed to put this knowledge into practice; they possessed knowledge about God but remained ignorant! Such ignorance is described in 2 Kings 17:27-41. That ignorance was encouraged by their self-willed arrogance. "However, they did not listen, but they did according to their earlier custom. So while these nations feared the Lord, they also served their idols" (17:40-41).

JOHN L. KACHELMAN JR.

2. Modern man has a greater revelation of the Lord God Almighty than Israel had at the foot of Mt. Sinai. We have the complete revelation of God in the Bible. The Bible provides us with all that we need to know to be pleasing to God (2 Peter 1:3).

Yet there are those who think they can improve on the revelation of "all things that pertain to life and godliness." They want to *rethink* biblical doctrine, *refashion* biblical worship and *redesign* the biblical God. They imagine they are wise enough to remake God so that He will be more "acceptable" in our modern world.

The arrogance of such people is shocking. Such should be confronted with righteous anger and immediate calls for repentance (Acts 8:18-23). Sadly such are never confronted. Often just the opposite, they are coddled because no one wants to upset them. But such coddling only allows them to continue in their idolatrous ways and corrupt the congregation!

C. 🖑 **Devout obedience to God's Word and not to man's imaginations about what is "better"**—"Then all the people tore off the gold rings which were in their ears and brought *them* to Aaron. He took *this* from their hand, and fashioned it with a graving tool and made it into a molten calf" (Exodus 32:3-4).

1. Israel had pledged to obey God and keep His covenant (Exodus 19:1-8). But that vow of commitment was not kept. Quickly the promise was forgotten and the focus of their faith was changed.

2. Sadly we see this same development today. Many are too eager and quickly forfeit the assurance that comes from faithfulness to God's commands. They have given up God's blessed assurance for the fleeting emotional responses that come from man's redesigns in faith, practice and worship.

Too many Church leaders are taking ideas and blurred beliefs and fashioning them into a modern idol that replaces God. And the justification is that it "improves" the Church, opens up opportunities to save souls, invigorating the worship, and making Christianity "more meaningful." But peal back the justifications and all you find is an erring idolatry. No Truth supports their efforts.

This calamity has often occurred (Galatians 1:6; 5:7).

When you obeyed the gospel you vowed to the Lord God Almighty that you would remain steadfast because you recognized Christ as Lord and Savior. How does one explain away his vow of commitment? How does one throw away steadfast loyalty to God's commands and accept selfish standards? And the amazing fact to consider is that there is no realization on that part of those involved that God is being redesigned—they are totally deluded. They believe they are doing right! But they are going to be confronted with a damning message (Matthew 7:21-23).

And those who do not challenge these modern idolaters share the guilt and grief for the compromise that brings chaos to the Lord's Church—especially elders, preachers, and teachers!

D. 🖰 **Leaders who are strong and openly zealous for God, not complacent and compromising**—"Now when Aaron saw *this*, he built an altar before it; and Aaron made a proclamation and said, 'Tomorrow *shall be* a feast to the LORD'" (Exodus 32:5).

1. Aaron was the appointed leader in Moses' absence. It was his responsibility to govern and control. It was his duty to make certain the people maintained their vow of commitment to the Lord God Almighty. His responsibility is evident in the way that Moses challenged Aaron to be accountable for what had happened.

   Instead of being a bold and strong leader, Aaron was weak and complicit in the sin of idolatry. As the leader, Aaron was responsible for the chaos.

2. It is incredulous to see this same error repeated in the Lord's Church today! Today the Lord's Church is often compromised because the leaders (elders, preachers, and teachers) are not strong and zealous for God's commands.

Many think that a passive attitude is best and so they timidly sit while the modern idolaters work their evil and corrupt the congregation.

Elders are to be bold and courageous (Titus 1:9). Elders are the *shepherds* of the congregation and that metaphor communicates that they are to guard, protect, fight off danger, and nurture the health of the congregation. A complacent and compromising shepherd is inacceptable!

"Son of man, prophesy against the shepherds of Israel. Prophesy and say...'Woe, shepherds of Israel...My flock has become a prey, My flock has even become food for all the beasts of the field for lack of a shepherd, and My shepherds did not search for My flock, but rather the shepherds fed themselves and did not feed My flock'...Thus says the Lord GOD, 'Behold, I am against the shepherds, and I will demand My sheep from them...'" (Ezekiel 34:2, 8-10).

Christians--especially the leaders--are to be steadfast and unmovable (1 Corinthians 15:58). We are to stand firm and never retreat regarding God's revealed commands (1 Timothy 1:18-19).

Conclusion

In our next lesson we will continue listing the remaining eight responses that God expects His People to demonstrate whenever they are in the presence of those seeking to redesign God and His commands.

- 9 -

Guarding the Reverence (Pt. 2)

(Exodus 32:1-5)

Introduction

I. ✒ In our previous lesson we saw that the greatest religious danger we face and the most lethal and cunning evil Satan utilizes is "apathy." ✒ A probing question asks, "Am I guilty?" This insidious evil is subtle and it is seldom realized until too late. Apathy has led to the devastation of civilizations and to the Lord's Church.

It was this deadly apathy that destroyed Israel; the people became unconcerned and insensitive to the presence of evil idolatry. The Lord's Church is often the unsuspecting victim as congregational members are content to drift along resting in a false assurance that things are going well.

In the time of the Judges apathy was responsible for Israel being uninvolved and unconcerned. ✒ It was this apathy that drew God's harsh judgment in Judges 5:23: "'Curse Meroz,' said the angel of the LORD, 'Utterly curse its inhabitants; because they did not come to the help of the LORD, to the help of the LORD against the warriors.'"

II.   In this lesson we return to the gold calf idolatry event at Sinai (Exodus 32) and discover directions for modern man on how he must react to modern idolatry. Only this behavior will be pleasing to God and only these actions will confront the evil of modern idolatry's redesign of God's character and doctrine.

We have already noticed four of these actions that God expects to be demonstrated whenever His People are in the presence of idolatry that seeks to refashion, redesign and rethink the revealed commands of the Almighty God. God does not want an apathetic reaction. God wants immediate action; He expects confrontation. The gold calf event clearly reveals what God expects His People to do.

Body

I.   🖰 God's expectations of His People when idolatry is present.

What do you do when you witness people redesigning God's commands so the commands are "more exhilarating" and "more meaningful"? Do you sit mumbling your objections in whispered tones? No! That is not the response God expects His dedicated People to demonstrate. Passivity, compromise, and timidity are NOT what the Almighty God expects from those who sincerely seek Him.

From the gold calf event we discover twelve points that offer instruction on how we must deal with idolatry. These twelve points highlight responses God expects to be seen in His Church as modern idolaters seek to modify and change the revealed commands and patterns.

In our previous lesson we considered *four actions* that God expects when His People are facing idolatrous temptations:

A. Courage and not cowering

B. Education in Truth and not enabling error from ignorance

C. Devout obedience to God's Word and not to man's imaginations about what is "better"

D. Leaders who are strong and openly zealous for God not complacent and compromising

II. Continue looking at the gold calf incident and observe *eight more* actions that God expects His People to demonstrate as they confront and conquer idolatry.

A. Holy reverence and not worldly emotionalism—"they rose early and offered burnt offerings, and brought peace offerings; and the people sat down to eat and to drink, and rose up to play" (Exodus 32:6).

1. Idolatry is all about feeling and emotionalism. The Israelites were operating on their own knowledge and feelings (32:1b). They sought emotions and feelings and they fashioned what they wanted (32:6). They were operating on THEIR desires and not on God's.

2. Today's modern idolaters are like ancient Israel. They seek emotions and feelings as validation for their practices. If something makes them "feel" different then it is considered valid. All things are redefined and new actions are concocted to pull emotional triggers and make the worship "more meaningful."

BUT, it is not a holy reverence. It is worldly emotionalism. Such a position totally ignores godly reverence. Those seeking feelings to make "worship more meaningful and exhilarating" are flagrantly ignoring Inspiration's command in Hebrews 12:28 and have shut their eyes and ears to the Truth of Hebrews 12:29!

The problem with emotionalism is that at first the desired "wow!" is achieved but then there is an emotional saturation and no longer does the person feel the "electrical wow!" And then the emotional scale must be kicked up a notch so the feelings return...and so develops the devolving cycle of idolatry's emotionalism. Idolatry vainly seeks feelings from DOING.

God's Truth is not validated by mankind's fickle emotions. God's Truth offers an amazing joy, a peace that passes all understanding, and a contentment that is divine. God's Truth provides assured feelings from KNOWLEDGE (Galatians 5:22-25; 1 John 5:13).

B. Confrontation and not silence—"Go down at once, for your people, whom you brought up from the land of Egypt, have corrupted *themselves.*" (32:7).

1. Idolatry could not be ignored; it could not be swept under the rug. There had to be a blunt confrontation. It was evil. It was ungodly. It sought to lead away from God's Truth. Moses had no choice. He was commanded by God to go and confront those who sought to compromise God's commands and remake the divine Sovereign into an image of a cow!

2. This need for confronting compromise has never been eliminated. God has always demanded that His People confront error and make sure the redesigns of God's commands are not tolerated.

The elders must not hesitate to "silence" those who are rebellious to God's commands (Titus 1:9-11). The elders are to "hold fast" the "sound doctrine" and by doing this they are to "silence" those who seek to change God's structure and commands (described by Inspiration as "rebellious men, empty talkers and deceivers"). Elders have been given a divine charge to confront those who try to bring in a redesigned religious practice!

The preachers and teachers have a duty to confront and condemn those who seek to redesign God's structure and commands (1 Timothy 1:3-7; 2 Timothy 4:1-5). It is tempting for these to shirk from offering a rebuke that is needed (2 Timothy 1:7).

C. 🕊 **Exclusiveness and not assimilation**—"They have quickly turned aside from the way which I commanded them" (32:8; see also 2 Chronicles 19:2; 20:35-37.)

1. Israel had committed to an exclusive union with God (Exodus 19:3-8). There is no confusion. They recognized God as "the **LORD**." This title refers to the uniqueness and sovereignty of God. It asserts there is only ONE "**LORD**." As Israel committed to a covenant with this one God she vowed to exclude all unions with any other gods. But listen to God's words— "they have quickly turned aside."

The problem was that the nation was still holding onto the polytheism of Egypt. They were willing to follow whatever "god" was needed at the moment. So at Sinai's foot they assented to obey the ONE "**LORD**" but as the days passed so did their passion. They were lured back into the philosophy of pagan idolatry. The Exclusive demands of the Almighty seemed less thunderous and the consent of the nation faded.

2. This is sadly repeated throughout mankind's history with God. There are Christians who agree to the exclusive covenant with the Lord God Almighty, but then their passion ebbs and their commitment fades. Eventually, they fail to honor the exclusive agreement (Hebrews 3:12-14; Revelation 2:4).

Modern idolatry seeks to remake God in our image so that His laws and expectations of exclusiveness are no longer binding. Today there is the idolatrous objective that "Each can find God in his own way." Others suggest that it is permissible for each to follow God's leadings however they are personalized.

An open fellowship is encouraged where all expressions and actions of worship and faith are accepted and none are condemned. When this happens, modern idolatry has succeeded in remaking God into our image of what "God" is to be!

The exclusive nature of God may be uncomfortable but it is a non-negotiable aspect of His character. Pluralism does not fit our exclusive God.

Why is the Church ashamed of upholding its EXCLUSIVENESS—they are God's Holy People, God's Holy Priests, and God's Holy Kingdom. And yet they act as if they are ashamed to proclaim the bold assertion that the Apostles proclaimed—"only ONE" (Acts 4:12; Ephesians 4:4-6).

"We tend to concentrate negatively on how embarrassingly different we are rather than on how commendably distinctive we are" (Smith, 107)

This exclusiveness is not only an unalterable part of God but it is an immovable part of His covenant with mankind.

God has only ONE way that things are to be done—it is His way and His way only. God has never permitted mankind to tweak the divine commands. From the construction of the Tabernacle, to the purity of His People, to the character and integrity of His Church God has required man to demonstrate an utter exclusiveness—do it the way He specified!

God's exclusiveness is seen in His commands. He has specified what He wants man to do. Silence regarding expressions or beliefs in religious devotion is NOT license for man doing whatever he wishes to do to make religion "more meaningful."

Modern idolatry ignores this exclusive principle. In fact, not only must modern idolatry ignore the principle of exclusiveness, modern idolatry must remove it in order to lure people into its false doctrines!

Read again these comments that seek to invalidate God's exclusiveness and allow man to remake God in his own image:

"Our God has strange taste for He loves Rejoicing, Spontaneity, and Graciousness. He enjoys watching His children have fun and enjoy themselves...If He didn't specifically command it then it must not be important to Him and we should find freedom in permission to do the uncommanded" (Notes 1:12-13).

"If the Bible is silent on what we want to do then we are free to do it!" Note this comment: *"Where Scripture is silent, certainly someone has to decide what is expedient—that ought to be left to the decision makers who are having to ask, 'What is needed NOW?'"* (Notes 7:11).

"God wired all of us differently...BE OURSELVES—to worship God in our own unique and different way. We can then use the gifts and special wiring that God placed in each of us" (Notes 7:14). Here is the foundation of modern idolatry—each is permitted to do as he chooses—no definite commanded actions or expressions—all is permitted, nothing is wrong. If you want "authority" then simply ask one of the "Leaders" in the congregation who will give you permission.

D. 🖐 **Anger and not passive surrender**—"Now then let Me alone, that My anger may burn against them and that I may destroy them" (32:10); " Moses' anger burned" (32:19).

1. The emotion of anger is demonstrated by the Almighty God and Moses. Moses is known as the "meekest" of all men (Numbers 12:3) yet here is action that many think is the antithesis of meekness. Moses was angry. He was incensed. He was livid with rage.

   Anger was *justified.*

2. It is a sad commentary on the compromised Church that this anger is missing in today's Church. It is a righteous wrath that erupts because the divine commands have been polluted by man's selfishness. It is an emotional expression because God's holiness has been treated with a casual indifference.

   There are times when it is sinful NOT to be angry! When people attempt to *remake* God, *refashion* God's structures, or *rethink* God's commands, or *redesign* God's worship expressions and actions—it is time to become as incensed as Moses. But today there is seldom even a whimper that escapes.

Too many seek to avoid the anger of man by ignoring the anger of God.

There is an inevitable conflict between righteousness and ungodliness that OUGHT to ignite angry emotions from God's People.

You are going to make someone angry. WHO will you anger? Will it be God or those who are trying to refashion God? Far too many compromise the immortal principles of Holy Scripture for "peace." But "peace at any price" is too expensive!

Stephen made a choice to face man's anger rather than God's (Acts 7:54). Paul refused to "moderate" his preaching even if he angered those who heard him (Galatians 4:16). Jeremiah's lament was that Judah refused to choose to follow God and in an angry query pointed out that their apathy led to its destruction (Lamentations 1:12).

What makes you angry? Anger is an emotion that releases all restraints and you clearly see one as he is. There is a truism that states, "If you want to understand a person's character, find out what makes that person laugh, what makes him weep, and what makes him angry."

God is watching His People to see if they will demonstrate anger toward those who compromise His righteousness.

Righteousness anger is controlled by the Scriptures (Psalm 106:19-22). Moses was angry because a group had taken the glory of the Almighty God and treated it as if it was trash!

How angry do you become when a group takes the glory of God, His commands, His worship, His exclusive covenant and treats them as if they are nothing but disposables? They treat the Almighty as if He was garbage! This is exactly what modern idolatry does in the Lord's Church.

Sometimes it is a sin NOT to be angry.

When is the last time you were incensed because some modern idolater tried to force a redesign of the Almighty God upon you and others?

E. 🖐 **Boldness and not reticence**—"He took the calf which they had made and burned it with fire, and ground it to powder, and scattered it over the surface of the water and made the sons of Israel drink it" (32:20).

"Now when Moses saw that the people were out of control—for Aaron had let them get out of control to be a derision among their enemies—then Moses stood in the gate of the camp..." (32:25-26).

1. There was a great commotion in the Israeli camp. Confusion and chaos governed. There was no order. Such an environment would be intimidating. But Moses did not hesitate. He acted with a commanding boldness to arrest the actions of those who were treating the glory of the Almighty God as if it was nothing special. As soon as Moses saw what was happening he "took," "burned," "ground," "scattered," "made," "stood," and "called."

    No hesitation. No intimidation to avoid confrontation because "some may leave" or "some will get their feelings hurt."

    The focused concern was God's glory! Moses cared only for the glory of God. That concern was unmistakable. And to be sure he was not misunderstood, he called for those on the Lord's side to join him.

2. The boldness of Moses stands in marked contrast with many today that are hesitant and timid to confront those who are redesigning God's commands for worship and salvation.

    Today there seems to be a greater concern for those guilty of remaking God in their image than there is for the glory of God. How can one justify such an insult to the Almighty?

Christ makes it clear that our number one priority; our supreme focus; our consuming objective is to uphold God's glory rather than man (Matthew 10:32-39).

Some object, "But if we offend them they might leave and never come back." In response we ask, "And exactly WHOM do you want to offend...one who is showing a total disregard for the glory of God and encouraging others to do the same or the Almighty God of heaven? You will offend someone...so WHO do you choose?"

Moses did not hesitate about that choice.

F. ✒ **Separation from idolaters and not association and encouragement**—"Moses stood in the gate of the camp, and said, 'Whoever is for the LORD, *come* to me!'" (32:26).

1. Moses wanted the national unity of Israel to remain intact. Moses looked at the nation and he saw God's own possession; a kingdom of priest; a holy nation (Exodus 19:5-6). Moses had consecrated the nation as a whole nation to the Lord (Exodus 19:14). I imagine that never once did Moses think the people would suffer division because they had pledged their commitment to God's covenant.

   But separation came. Idolatry arose and when left unchecked it pulled a number away from their consecration. The flagrant rejection of God's commands brought the division into a sharp focus. There was one group devoted to following God. There was one group devoted to rejecting God. The separation could not be bridged.

   Moses called for people to make a choice—no middle ground and no grey areas. You are either FOR God or AGAINST God.

2. This separation is required today. We are called to make a choice...will we uphold and support those who wish to refashion God's commands for

100

salvation and worship or will we stand firm with those who are committed to following God's revealed will in the Bible?

A choice has to be made. You cannot postpone the choice. You cannot remain neutral in the matter. You are on one side or the other.

The ancient call is not limited to the Mt. Sinai event. Today the question is urgently asked, "Who is for the Lord?"

3. It is a sad that even though the question is as valid today as at Sinai, many refuse to see the urgency. They refuse to take sides; they claim they are neither "for" nor "against" either side. They seek neutrality. But Scripture teaches us that neutrality is not possible.

   a. Those that endorse evil must be called out (3 John 9-11).

   b. Divisions MUST exist (1 Corinthians 11:19).

   c. Sides must be chosen (Matthew 12:30).

G. ✋ **Action and not immobility**—"Moses stood in the gate of the camp" (32:26).

1. Moses "stood." This Hebrew term is illustrative of Moses attitude and actions on that eventful day. It comes from the Hebrew term עָמַד (âmad, *aw-mad'*). It indicates that one has taken a firm position and is continuing in that position; he is unmoved; he dwells there; he endures; he is established securely; and he will not be moved.

These words show that Moses had positioned himself and would not move. He was going to remain there. He would continue in that position—no moving; no modifying!

2. This steadfast attitude marks many heroes of the Bible. These "stood" and they were not going to be moved. Nothing would move them from their position. Their stubborn resolve was because of their faith in God and their determination to guard the glory of God.

Phinehas is a good illustration of this. Phinehas "stood" and chose to guard the glory of God at Baal-peor (Numbers 25:3-15). Even though the leaders at Peor were inactive, Phinehas acted! At Peor the congregation was wringing their hands and shaking their heads and saying "I cannot believe this is happening here." Phinehas acted! (Numbers 25:3-8).

3. Christians are commanded to "stand" (Ephesians 6:11, 13, 14).

How strong is your resolve to imitate Moses, Phinehas, and other Christians who have chosen to "stand" for God and actively confront the modern idolaters? Let us remain immobile in the truth when we see God's glory being compromised!

When leaders are doing nothing; when the congregation is wringing their hands and shaking their heads and saying "I cannot believe this is happening here," YOU need to act. Be as heroic as Phinehas and you will be blessed by God for standing for Truth and the glory of God (Numbers 25:10-13).

H. ☞ **Clarity in understanding and not confusion**—"He said to them, 'Thus says the Lord, the God of Israel'... So the sons of Levi did as Moses instructed" (32:27, 28).

1. Moses confronted those seeking to redesign God with the Word of God. It was a "thus says the Lord" that formed the authority for his actions that day.

2. Christians need to understand that the authority for what we do in religious devotion must be from the Word of God. We are to speak as God's revelation speaks (1 Peter 4:11).

Whatever we do in teaching, in actions, in expressions MUST rest upon a "Thus says the Lord"!

If someone wants to suggest a "new" expression or action or teaching, then let him offer it with a clear exegesis from the New Testament!

Changes and innovations are not to be allowed because they "promise" to make our worship "more meaningful." Such is the criteria for idolatry NOT the holy God.

We look for authority in our expressions and activities and beliefs--NOT from the Elders or preacher or teachers or some group within the congregation. We look for authority in our expressions, activities and beliefs to the pages of the New Testament. The ultimate test is the question, "What does the Scripture say?" (Romans 4:3a).

If the Scriptures are silent, then that expression, action or belief is NOT authorized by God; if one proceeds in satisfying self, he is guilty of idolatry and will be damned by God (1 Corinthians 4:6).

How sad that modern idolatry has convinced so many they can be pleasing to God without Scriptural authority. Instead of basing their expressions, beliefs and actions on the Bible's authority, they use "good feelings" and "excitement and happiness" as their foundation.

This philosophy did not justify the idolaters at Sinai or those from Sinai to the close of the Old Testament or even those under the New Testament Scriptures (Matthew-Revelation).

III. Focused Lessons Learned

A. 🖱 God expects Christians to stand on His side confronting those confusing and compromising Truth.

B. 🖱 God holds Leaders responsible for their sin in allowing man to remake God in their image.

C. 🖱 God never exempts or excuses man from strict obedience.

D. 🖱 God never applauds those who compromise with error.

Conclusion

As this lesson concludes, let us focus on a few final emphases from our study:

I.   God cannot be redesigned even if certain aspects of Him are uncomfortable! We must guard against both extremes--redesigning God by going "beyond" what is written and redesigning God by "limiting" what is written—allowing attitudes and actions to form that are contrary to God's will (2 Kings 18:4).

One may deny the principles, examples and commands of Bible Truth BUT that denial does not erase the obligation for them to obey all of God's Truth! "Not everyone...but he that doeth the will of My Father in heaven" (Matthew 7:21-23).

II.   Compromise is capitulation! Compromise of God's biblical Truth does not yield peace but only a slow eroding of biblical Truth that eventually results in no absolute Truth of the Bible being recognized regardless of how abhorrent it is.

A. An interesting irony is found in modern idolatry. Bible doctrine is understood and is believed by the individual until idolatry's evil infects and then the Christian begins to seek to do things his way instead of God's way. At that point the modern idolater has to rethink, redefine, and reconceptualize that which was established and understood for years.

B. These pride themselves in the "god of understanding" and were described by Inspiration as becoming visible in the grievous last days:

"For men will be lovers of self, lovers of money, boastful, arrogant, revilers, disobedient to parents, ungrateful, unholy, unloving, irreconcilable, malicious gossips, without self-control, brutal, haters of good, treacherous, reckless, conceited, lovers of pleasure rather than lovers of God, holding to a form of godliness, although they have denied its power; Avoid such men as these. For among them are those who enter into households and captivate weak women weighed down with sins, led on by various impulses, always learning and never able to come to the knowledge of the truth. Just as Jannes and Jambres opposed

Moses, so these men also oppose the truth, men of depraved mind, rejected in regard to the faith" (2 Timothy 3:2-8).

C. Notice specifically that ☞ Inspiration says those who are guilty of such heinous evils are those who will not submit to the simple authority of God's Scriptures. These always have to find an explanation around the commands of God. They are "always learning and never able to come to the knowledge of the truth...of depraved mind, rejected in regard to the faith" (2 Timothy 3:8).

III. Let us close by emphasizing the certain fact...☞ God's Leaders are accountable for their shepherding! (See the judgment of God upon Israel's leaders at Baal-Peor in Numbers 25:40.)

Jeremiah 50:6: "My people have become lost sheep; their shepherds have led them astray. They have made them turn aside...And have forgotten their resting place."

Ezekiel 34:1-10: "Son of man, prophesy against the shepherds of Israel. Prophesy and say to those shepherds, 'Thus says the Lord GOD, "Woe, shepherds of Israel who have been feeding themselves! Should not the shepherds feed the flock?...My flock has become a prey, My flock has even become food for all the beasts of the field for lack of a shepherd, and My shepherds did not search for My flock, but *rather* the shepherds fed themselves and did not feed My flock...'Thus says the Lord GOD, "Behold, I am against the shepherds, and I will demand My sheep from them and make them cease from feeding sheep. So the shepherds will not feed themselves anymore, but I will deliver My flock from their mouth, so that they will not be food for them."'"

IV. Being surrounded by modern idolatry is discouraging. When worshipping assemblies are turned into raucous gatherings where God's glory is totally absent, it is disheartening. Such is a devilish enticement for us to surrender and quit. If you feel that way, you are not alone. Elijah struggled with the same evils. He was ready to quit; but God reminded him that as bad as things seemed, the way of righteousness was still strong.

ᗩ Idolatry may be so common that we think all is lost; but at those times we need to "stand" fixed with the confidence that God gave Elijah: "Yet I will leave 7,000 in Israel, all the knees that have not bowed to Baal and every mouth that has not kissed him" (1 Kings 19:18).

V.   There are two illustrations with which we close this lesson. ᗩ Both of these urge a committed fidelity to following God. But each also stresses that we all have a choice—whose side will we take?

A. 1 Samuel 17—David & Goliath:

David came into the Israeli war camp at a frightening moment. The troops were cowering in fear. The glory of Jehovah God was being cursed. The pagan idols were being viewed as omnipotent and their followers as invincible. The narrative describes the tragic situation that arises when God's People refuse to uphold the divine Majesty and confront those who follow idols.

But young David refused to join those who were cowering and intimidated. He did not sit silently and bemoan the dreadful situation facing the nation. David refused to allow the majestic glory and supreme authority of Jehovah to be refused. His choice was to stand for God. Read the narrative and highlight his heroic words. These ought to be on the lips and in the hearts of every Christian today which sees modern idolatry.

"David said to the Philistine, 'You come to me with a sword, a spear, and a javelin, but I come to you in the name of the Lord of hosts, the God of the armies of Israel, whom you have taunted. This day the Lord will deliver you up into my hands...that all the earth may know that there is a God in Israel, and that all this assembly may know that the Lord does not deliver by sword or by spear; for the battle is the Lord's and He will give you into our hands'" (1 Samuel 17:45-47).

B. The Potter and the clay:

Isaiah spoke to a nation of God's People that had redesigned, refashioned, rethought, and reconceptualized "god." They had remade God into their own image. So the prophet struggled with trying to reason with the idolatrous nation and persuade them to return to God (Isaiah 1:16-20). Isaiah presented the people with a metaphor showing they had a choice. The message spoken then speaks even in our modern time to those seeking to redesign God's commands so the commands are "more meaningful."

The way God designed the divine plan...

Isaiah sought to persuade Israel to understand that God has absolute authority and, therefore, they had no option except obeying exactly as God commanded. "But now, O Lord, You are our Father, We are the clay, and You our potter; and all of us are the work of Your hand" (Isaiah 64:8).

The way modern idolatry has corrupted the divine plan...

Unfortunately, the people refused to acknowledge God's authority and obey exactly as God commanded. They thought they were above God and able to redesign some commands, lessen loyalty, and reject God's exclusiveness. To this attitude the Prophet spoke these words trying to persuade the people that such actions and attitudes were blasphemy: "You turn things around! Shall the potter be considered as equal with the clay, That what is made would say to its maker, 'He did not make me'; Or what is formed say to him who formed it, 'He has no understanding'?" (Isaiah 29:16). Note the phrase "turn things around" (from ...הֹפֶךְ hôphek ho'-fek; an *upset*, that is, *perversity:* - turning of things upside down). This indicates that Israel had chosen to look at what God commanded and then redesign it so that all was contrary to the divine expectations.

C. We have a choice. Let us choose to guard the reverence that ought to be demonstrated for our Holy God!

- 10 -

Standing For The Lord

(Hebrews 12:28-29)

Introduction

I.   The tragedy of man remaking God into his own image is evident. Surrounding the faithful Christians are multitudes seeking to lessen the authority of the Almighty God by depreciating the reverence and awe that ought to be seen (Hebrews 12:28, 29).

What is to be our reaction to the tragic cultural pluralism that refuses to honor the sovereign majesty and commanding authority of the great God of heaven? Do we sit in silence as cunning and crafty minds seek to compromise the Lord's Church and moderate the Lord's commands? No! We are challenged to confront, expose and rebuke such efforts (2 Timothy 4:1-5).

🖐 The Epistle to the Ephesians comes to a close with Inspiration's "call to arms for the Lord's Church." The Epistle to the Ephesians highlights the Lord's Church with the sublime words, metaphors, and commands. According to the Ephesian Epistle there is no other religious organization comparable with the church of Christ! The church of Christ is unique because of a number of factors: Christ is its

Head; the members comprise the Body; salvation is exclusively reserved for those who are members of the church of Christ; unity in doctrine and consideration in relationships distinctively mark those who are members of the church of Christ. Ephesians presents the Lord's Church as the ideal environment of the saved while alive on earth.

A. Modern Idolaters arrogantly offer a pitiful substitute to replace God's divine plan but it does not work! Some shamelessly seek to "tweak" and modify the unique nature and doctrines of the Lord's Church but they fail. Some like to "think outside the box" and claim they have a "culturally relevant church" as they presume to think their knowledge is superior to the Lord God Almighty. But their folly leads to eternal damnation.

B. The Epistle to the Ephesians concludes with an alarm calling the readers to action. One has described this call by this phrase: "The words ring short and sharp as a bugle-call." This alarm deserves our attention.

C. After Paul's sublime discussion on the constitution, nature and glorious destiny of the church of Christ, we are somberly reminded that formidable spiritual foes are present. The Lord's Church cannot avoid contention. Strong evil forces are all around and Believers must understand they are powerless by themselves—their strength is utterly insufficient but the Lord's power is offered in exceeding abundance (Ephesians 3:20). When Paul sent Timothy to Ephesus, these exhortations were given which urge the Ephesians and all other Christians to STAND:

1. 1 Timothy 1:10. *Some will violently oppose you in teaching God's Truth—but STAND!* Paul begins the letter to Timothy with an immediate reference to the crisis of false teachers. Paul observes that anyone who really loves the Truth of God cannot tolerant religious error. Paul impresses Timothy that there are things contrary to sound doctrine and these must be addressed. The term "contrary" is interesting to study. It is a compound word (ἀντίκειμαι antikeimai) literally meaning "to lie against." The term presents the image of active opposition (Galatians 5:17). The word suggests a strong

refusal (2 Thessalonians 2:4). Thus, Timothy was exhorted by Paul to realize that one teaching sound doctrine will face a stubborn and active opposition.

2. 1 Timothy 6:3. *Some will never agree with you—but STAND!* Paul exposes the motives of those who refuse sound doctrine. These are ruled by selfishness instead of humble commitment to God. These are puffed up, know nothing, constantly bicker and fuss about trivial points, are corrupted in mind, are ignorant of the Truth, and seek only self-centered gains. There will be those who refuse to consent to sound teaching. "Consent" is from προσέρχομαι (proserchomai) meaning that one is willing to "come to an agreement" with another. Thus, Paul tells Timothy that regardless of what is done, some will never agree with sound doctrine. This will be a discouraging fact for those who love the Truth and strive to preach/teach it.

3. 2 Timothy 1:13. *Some will urge you to lessen your convictions and moderate your beliefs and redefine God's doctrine—but STAND!* Only those who hold to sound doctrine will find reward on the Judgment Day (1:12b). Emphasized in this verse is the necessity of remaining sound in one's belief and practice and transmitting sound doctrine in one's teaching. Paul stresses the attitude with which one is to show respect for sound doctrine. One is to hold fast to sound doctrine. "Hold" is from the Greek ἔχω (echo), which refers to one holding onto a mental concept. Such a one is convinced of the concept and will not change his mind (i.e. will not let go). The stress is upon steadfast adherence. This term is at times used as a metaphor of warfare stressing the tenacity of troops as they fight against strong opponents. To what is one to demonstrate this stubborn adherence? To the pattern of sound words. This was the example of teaching and practice of religious beliefs that Paul had demonstrated. Thus, Timothy was commanded to do things exactly as Paul had done these things. There is no room for redesigning the pattern.

D. There is an empowering strength available—BUT it is found ONLY "in the Lord" (Ephesians 6:10). Those who are a part of Christ's Body (the Church) have access to this strength. God will overcome His enemies. God does not need our strength to overcome, *but* we need His strength for we cannot defend ourselves without His power! Thus, in order to enjoy the sublime blessings that have been described in chapters 1-5, Christians MUST be strong in the Lord and STAND in the power of His might!

II. Heroic "stands" have been chronicled throughout the pages of history. These bring to light the zeal and commitment that mankind has to basic principles in their commitment which brings blessings to their lives.

A. All remember the 300 Spartans at Thermopylae whose brave stand against the superior numbers of Xerxes' Persian army and navy, provided opportunity for Greece to set proper defenses against invasion.

B. The heroic "stand"" of Admiral Lord Nelson on board the *HMS Victory* at Trafalgar is etched in the historical records of the Napoleonic Wars as the most significant naval battle where France and Spain lost 22 ships while the British lost none.

C. "Remember the Alamo" calls to memory the 189 brave men whose "last stand" won independence for Texas by uniting the Republic into an invincible army.

D. An account from World War 1 is most impressive. Field Marshal Sir Douglas Haig, British commander issued what became known as the "Backs to the Wal" order April 11, 1917 when the Germans launched a frightening artillery bombardment from its Bruchmuller battering train. *"With our backs to the wall and believing in the justice of our cause, each one of us must fight on to the end...Every position must be held to the last man. There must be no retirement"* (Keegan, 405).

E. The ancient Israelites witnessed a heroic stand against idolatry at Peor, and Phinehas rose to greatness because of his dedication to God.

III. Paul's pen of Inspiration makes a blunt point...Christians are called by Inspiration to make and hold a "last stand" on earth's spiritual battlefield. Our backs are against the wall—we have no other option! The sublime constitution, nature and glorious eternity offered to us in the Lord's Church will be decided in our "stand."

Body

I. **"Stand in the Lord"**—*Its challenges*

A. ✋ There is a challenge for the members of the church of Christ to acknowledge the divine doctrines regarding the Lord's Church (Ephesians 1:1-4:16).

1. The pointed application is simple. Do NOT relent, do NOT release, do NOT redefine the holy doctrine of the New Testament! Stand firm against anyone trying to change the New Testament pattern or accept compromise in order to have "peace."

2. The Greek term (ἵστημι, histēmi) translated as "stand" means: cease from movement; be in a stationary position; to stand still and not move; do not relent in resisting; remain stable; to stand fast; to persist; opposed to running away.

3. This stubbornness is restricted by the term "in the Lord." The only stubbornness that is applauded by the Almighty God is the stubborn decision to do ONLY as God says (Joshua 24:15b; Acts 5:29, 42).

B. ✋ There is a challenge for the members of the church of Christ to acquire the distinctive character of those belonging to the Lord's Church (Ephesians 4:17-5:24).

C. ✋ There is a challenge for the members of the church of Christ to protect the church of Christ (Ephesians 5:25-6:20).

1. We have been blessed by God's grace allowing us to become a part of Christ's Body; we are a part of Christ's Bride! We have been provided with

the necessary "armor" that MUST be worn by the Christian in order to access this supply of strength.

2. ✎ How will we act when dangers confront the Body and Bride of Christ? Will we sit silently? Will we rationalize changes that pollute the divine Truth? Will we close our eyes and mouths because we are intimidated by those who are arrogant and boastful in their efforts to change the Lord's Church? (1 Corinthians 5:1-7; Romans 16:17, 18; Revelation 2:14-16, 20-23).

3. According to Scripture *nothing less* than a full, vigorous confrontation is acceptable to God (Acts 20:28-31a; 1 Timothy 1:3-8; 2 Timothy 1:7, 8; Ephesians 6:10, 11).

II. "Stand in the Lord"—*Its illustration*

The man who received the greatest commendation from God in the Old Testament for his "stand in the Lord" was not Abraham, Moses or David. He was a man who is seldom the subject of sermons, yet he single-handedly saved Israel and drew the highest endorsement from God. His name was *Phinehas*, and his story poignantly illustrates the words of Ephesians 6:10-20. Phinehas' heroic "stand" sprang out of pure, unsolicited, godly zeal. His reaction was genuine; God said that he acted with the Lord's jealousy.

A. ✎ The setting.

1. Towards the end of Israel's 40 years of wandering, battling and raising a new generation, the nation is now camped at the edge of Moab--just miles from the Jordan River--and waiting for the last Wilderness battle to begin. Once Moab is out of the way, they will ford the Jordan into the Promised Land.

2. In the previous 2 chapters (Numbers 23-24) Balak the King of Moab, afraid of the terrible defeat he will likely suffer at the hands of the invincible Israelites, hires Balaam (the false prophet of Midian) to curse Israel so that the Moabites can defeat them.

a. Four times Balaam tries to cast a binding curse over Israel, but each time God intervenes and informs Balaam that Israel is under His blessing and can neither be cursed nor defeated.

b. Balak (the Moabite King) is dejected until Balaam tells him that he has a way to defeat Israel without needing to curse them, or even fight them.

c. Balaam counsels Balak to extend peace to Israel; to send his young women and temple prostitutes among the Israeli men and let nature take its course. Balaam informs Balak that the God of Israel detests idolatry, and the Israelites can curse themselves before God with their own sin. They begin committing fornication, indulging their flesh and soon drift into the Moabite temples of Baal Peor, where they become a curse to God.

d. Balak took Balaam's advice. The seductive foreign policy worked flawlessly and became a famous satanic strategy throughout the Bible. In the New Testament, Jude referred to it as "the Deception of Balaam" (Jude 11). In His rebuke to the Church of Pergamos, God referred to this passivity towards the world as the "Doctrine of Balaam" (Revelation 2:14).

e. Within a very short span of time, Israel degraded its own position from unconquerable to completely vulnerable. Not only did they drive off the protective presence of God through their fornication, they also brought an insatiable plague upon themselves. Twenty-four thousand men died by the plague and there was no sign of it letting up, despite their cries of repentance. Sin had conquered what Satan's scheming could not.

f. We have never realized that our own propensities for lust have always been far more effective in destroying us than Satan could ever hope to be (James 1:14-15).

B. 🖰 The trap of "peace."

1. This deplorable slide into decadence happened without confrontation by those who should have quickly stepped forward and stopped things. But

tragically there were none that "stood"" for God's Truth. It seems that all wanted "peace" and were willing to NOT "stand in the Lord" for righteousness. Tragically, this same destructive compromise is all too common today—many want "peace" instead of "standing" for the Truth of God.

2. This generation of Israelites were about to be annihilated by their own sin just when they were ready to enter the Promised Land. But they thought they had found "peace."

3. After victoriously fighting countless battles, and right at the point where their greatest moment was to begin, they were defeated! They were being destroyed, not on the fields of battle, but in the paralyzing arms of "peace."

4. This story should send shivers down the spine of every sincere Christian. The fact is that this narrative is NOT preached long and strong from pulpits today is an indication that Satan is still working feverishly to conceal the doctrine of Balaam! (Amos 6:1).

5. As the warriors of Israel laid aside their swords and shields to transition from victory to vacation with those who "wanted peace," an enemy arose from within their own flesh. The Canaan Rest that was to be their reward lay just days ahead of them, BUT they made the fatal decision to take their relaxation in the arms of their enemy's daughters. They took off more than their clothes in order to get comfortable in this new arrangement of "peace." They stripped themselves of the armor of faithfulness to God and became vulnerable. Gone were the breastplate of righteousness and the shield of faith, and the girdle of Truth, all of which had struck fear in the hearts of their demon-worshipping enemies. The warriors of Jehovah God Almighty turned their backs on Jehovah and followed their new girlfriends into the temples of Baal and came out the enemies of God (James 4:4).

6. Judgment was coming and the sword of Israel was about to fall in defeat. This time the sword would not fall on the Midianites or Moabites, but upon themselves as they sought to slay the enemy within.

C.

🖰 The reaction.

1. Judgment from God had already begun in the form of a plague that claimed twenty-four thousand men.

   a. The plague demonstrated the serious consequences of breaking covenant with God.

   b. It showed that those who enjoy the benefits of His covenant and represent His name can become His enemies by desecrating His Name through their idolatry.

   c. Tragically, a more serious corruption had occurred as the leaders of Israel had emboldened the people in their sin. The leaders failed to STAND against the corruption! Whether through passivity towards the sin or personal participation in the sin, the leadership was responsible for the total breakdown of respect and loyalty to the Almighty God.

2. Further judgment came when God instructed Moses to do two things:

   a. He was to kill all the chiefs and hang their bodies up in public for the people to see. The Judges over the tribes were to kill every individual person who had committed fornication and idolatry with the Moabites.

   b. Leaders are responsible for the sins of those under their charge. When they allow or neglect to reprove or personally participate in the unrighteous acts they will be held accountable (Ephesians 5:11).

   c. One of the saddest faults of our modern culture (both secular and Christian) is that leaders have become dependent upon and look for affirmation from popularity with people rather than approval from God for their authority. Our nation has become "post-Christian" and many, even in the Church, do not know and respect the Almighty God. The standard is popularity instead of righteous zeal for the Lord.

1. When the population or congregation ceases to walk in covenant with God, they no longer allow their leaders to answer to God. They want them to agree with their own selfish agendas.

2. Every church, nation, and group who lives indifferently towards God's demands, will insist upon leaders who approve (or at the least do not condemn) their particular sins and corruptions and changes to God's revealed Will for worship and work. Man today does not seek leaders with moral integrity but leaders who are willing to become moral puppets!

3. Only God-fearing people tolerate leaders who answer to God. The rest demand moral puppets. Paul laid out the line of accountability in his instructions to Timothy regarding the responsibility of God's leaders (1 Timothy 4:16; 2 Timothy 4:1-5).

   a. Paul makes it clear that Christian leaders are directly accountable to God to maintain the standards He has set for His Church. The Church belongs to God and thus God commands what the Church is to do. It is the church _OF_ (belonging to) Christ! Brethren, if you rebel regarding that identity, forget the fear of any reproaches or threats by people and their groups about "leaving." Prepare yourself to meet God's judgment because you have failed to "stand."

   b. Several times through the Scriptures God tells His servants to steel their resolve to resist the backsliding tendencies of the people who do not find God's commands to be convenient or pleasing (1 Corinthians 15:58; Hebrews 3:1-4:1).

   c. It is abundantly clear that leaders owe their allegiance to God, no matter who objects to their loyalty and commitment to God in their decisions. King Saul was a typical example of a man who became cursed of God and plagued by devils because he looked to his popularity with people rather than his responsibility toward God in fulfilling his duties (1 Samuel 13:11; 1 Samuel 15:10-28).

4. The Chiefs of Israel were executed and hung because the people looked to them for a reaction but they saw no resistance. So now they would get to see just how much power these leaders had to condone their sins.

5. When Moses unleashed the Judges to slay everyone who committed fornication and idolatry with Moab, the message became frightfully clear-- You cannot use the bad example of leaders as an excuse for your own sin.

   a. If your leaders turn cowardly before God and those leaders allow you to rebel, God Himself will judge the treasonous leaders and you will stand for your own sin.

   b. You can never excuse yourself with the failures of your leaders. God sees right through the excuse and will never accept it.

6. Take this lesson and apply it to your own private life. YOU are Israel and the ideals, convictions, and principles that you have chosen in your own mind and heart will guide your life. If the principles of your choice fail to keep you honest before God or they condone the practices of unfaithfulness to God, then (just like the chiefs of Israel) they will not be able to excuse you from judgment.

   a. Self-deception is not ignorance; it is rebellion.

   b. If the ideals and thoughts that lead you are allowing you to rebel against God and giving you a false sense of security, you should replace those with the biblical principles and then attack the rebellion in your own life.

   c. The only refuge that idolatry, immorality, and rebellion have in the life of a Christian is the delusional thinking of permissiveness and the rationalization that somehow the eternal and unchangeable rules of God do not apply to you personally. Consequently you cannot "stand" on the unchanging Truth of God!

7. Utterly amazing is the fact that despite the plague and the execution of the leaders and the idolaters, the people did not stop receiving the daughters of Moab. However, and even more amazing, they called for repentance and began to weep and pray before the tabernacle of God. They were weeping

and in sorrow because of all the evil—but they did nothing more than weep and show sorrow!

D. 🖰 The utter blasphemy

1. Zimri was a young Israelite and the son of a prominent man.

   a. Although twenty-four thousand of his countrymen had died as a result of their idolatrous and licentious relations with the Moabite women, Zimri was unfazed by the rebuke.

   b. Even the execution of the leaders had not convinced Zimri that disobeying God's rules with these females was dangerous.

   c. The real shock is that despite the fact that the Judges were hunting down and slaying the men who were doing what Zimri was doing, this young man somehow felt insulated against all judgment.

2. He saw no wrong in his actions. But worse, he somehow believed that he had a privilege that exempted him from the judgment that everyone else was falling under. To him there was no respect and regard for the Law of God.

   a. There is no advantage in speculating as to why Zimri thought the way he did.

   b. The fact is that this man had a calloused heart and an elitist attitude.

   c. He paraded his Midianite girlfriend right into the middle of the assembly where everyone was weeping before the Lord!

E. 🖰 The inescapable application.

1. As bad as it is to have a calloused heart and an elitist attitude, the refusal of the modern Church to act decisively against the sins that threaten our fellowship with God is far worse!

2. Cozbi, the woman that Zimri brought on his arm to show off to his brothers, was not a common Moabitess. She was a Midianite woman and the daughter of a King. The Moabites were devil worshippers.

3. Balaam was the architect of the strategy to destroy Israel by leading them into fornication and idolatry with the Moabite women. Cozbi (as a royal) was no doubt part of the master plan to insure Israel's total collapse. And here was this young fool bringing her right into the special service where Israel had gathered to cry out to God.

4. There is an alarming message arising from all this.

   a. By His own admission, God would have allowed Israel to be completely destroyed. In spite of the loud weeping, an act of atonement had not been offered. Punishment would not stop them. Tears could not save them. If some action was not performed, the sin would continue to devastate and destroy!

   b. It is a frightening reality to consider–punishment does not stop the corrosive work of sin, and tears from us do not turn away God's wrath. Something else is needed.

   c. Many Christians, churches, and missions throughout history have been lost because compromise and corruption began its degrading work in God's people and only weeping and sorrow was seen.

   "A preacher was not going to allow any Sunday school teachers to compromise the standards of God's Word so he called one of his teachers into the study. It was the late 1950s and the teacher was none other than Willie Nelson. The preacher said, "Willie, either you quit playing in beer joints or else you quit teaching Sunday school." Nelson replied, "You must be nuts." But the minister did not back down. Nelson recalled, "He had to choose between satisfying the congregation—including the hypocrites—or siding with a musician who drank and smoked and cussed and picked his guitar and sang in dance halls. I decided to stay with the beer joints." Nelson also said, "The preacher sounded so wrong to me that I quit the Baptist Church." Willie Nelson's decision to choose the beer joints over the church led him to other avenues of religious thought. He noted, "I discovered a world full of people who believed in reincarnation. The King James Version of the

Bible was later written to cover up the fact that Jesus had discovered reincarnation. The Aquarian Gospel had a great impact on me. It explained everything to my satisfaction." Compromise never leads to an oasis, it just deceives you with a myriad of mirages (*Houston Chronicle,* Nov. 3, 1988).

d. There is only one thing that can stop the destruction and appease the righteous judgment. We must demonstrate ACTION to confront and rebuke this evil. It is one thing that all of us have the power to do!

5. Numbers 25:6. Moses and all Israel were gathered at the Tabernacle, weeping before God. Some probably wept over their terrible loss. Some probably wept in grief, pleading with God to stop the plague and judgment. Some may have even wept due to conviction.

a. The plague was not stopping and, apparently, neither was the sinning. There was great sorrow—people shook their heads and no doubt said "I cannot believe this!" They wept and muttered but did nothing else. Probably some said, "What is the use? What good will any action be to stop all of this?"

b. The contrast was amazing as Zimri and the Midianite woman paraded through the assembly during this outcry.

c. The crush of conviction (in Israel's weeping) and the callousness of sin (in Israel's continued fornication) met without any clash; no explosive reaction; NOTHING! All the sorrow was show. All of the muttering was without substance. All Israel did was weep and mutter. Israel did NOTHING and was facing certain destruction.

d. Where was the righteous reaction that God's People should have expressed? No wonder the plague did not stop! Why would it? The leaders had all been executed for not lifting a finger to stop the people's slide into idolatry, but apparently no one got the point. The remaining people just sat there unwilling to act.

e. There is a terrible delusion today among Christians who believe that as long as God sees the intent of our hearts that is what matters to Him. Thus, Christians can sit silently and let God look at the heart of the sinner—no speech, only silence! But when the Church spins off into idolatry, immorality, false doctrine, and unscriptural worship, (unless someone stands up to stop it) no amount of heart feeling is going to keep God's judgment away.

F. The heroic "stand" (Numbers 25:7-8; Psalm 106:30)

1. Many people have zeal. But true zeal, the righteous zeal of God, is a very rare thing.

2. It is far easier to deplore and weep and gnash one's teeth about the existence of evils than it is to throw oneself into active contention against them. The true zeal of God derives its fire--not from the interests of men, but from the interests of God. Righteous zeal stops the destruction of sin!

3. How many zealous Christians who are ambitious to have God's Presence in their midst truly hate the things that separate them from God? How many are righteous enough to separate themselves from that evil? Righteous zeal does not sit silently; it STANDS for the Lord's way!

4. Phinehas acted out of pure, unsolicited, godly zeal. His reaction was genuine. God said that Phinehas acted with the Lord's jealousy (Numbers 25:11).

   Phinehas "stood"—this Hebrew term is understood as translating the concept of "take a stand against, in opposition to;" "to make a stand; hold one's ground and not give way;" "to arise, appear, come on the scene at an opportune time" (Brown, 763-764).

5. Do you strive to speak and live so as to be the one to turn God's displeasure away and restore His favor? Do you act with righteous zeal?

   a. Where are the Christians who will act with the zeal of God against the compromises that alienate us from God's Presence?

b. We cannot get churches to admit to the spiritual atrocities, defections and fornications that they commit, much less organize a unified front against them. And among the Christians out in the world who boldly denounce things like homosexual behavior, you would be hard-pressed to find more than a handful who will denounce the lust for numbers and the exaltation of the congregation's name which goes on right in the church without anyone objecting.

c. *David Crenshaw made an interesting stand against immorality. He operated a seven-screen movie theater outside of Spartanburg, South Carolina. In August of 1998, he vowed to no longer show R-rated movies even if he went bankrupt doing so. There was strong community support of his position; but after the first month's ban, his attendance dropped from two thousand customers per week to just twelve hundred. To his surprise and disgust, the community was not as supportive as he first believed. He called off the ban five months later after an estimated loss of $20,000 in ticket sales. Crenshaw said, "I thought people cared more. Apparently they don't care much." He went on to say, "You can't make people want something they don't want. This whole thing has left me really cynical." A disappointed local minister wisely summarized the situation: "It does not surprise me that he did not get support. Basically, people say they want morals, but they want it for everybody but themselves." Are we weeping and wringing our hands over the deplorable state of our nation's moral decline while simultaneously supporting the production of immoral entertainment? We may not want morality as much as we think (Leadership, 15).*

d. Are we weeping and wringing our hands over the godless actions of so many in our families and communities but (unlike Phinehas) we are sitting in silence and doing NOTHING!

6. When Moses ordered the execution of the Chiefs for their complicity in the idolatry, he was following an order from God. When the Judges began slaying the men who committed fornication and idolatry, they were following

orders from Moses (who received the orders from God). They all acted. But none of them acted from pure jealousy for the Lord's glory.

7. But when Phinehas acted, he was not following an order nor was he obeying a specific scriptural edict. In this instance, Phinehas' heart beat as one with God's. How often do people leave the responsibility for zeal in the hands of "religious professionals" instead of accepting the fact they are personally responsible?

G. The highest commendation from God (Numbers 25:12, 13).

1. God extended a special covenant to Phinehas and his descendants to stand as intercessors for the people, before God, throughout their generations. This act is a significant honor and highlights just how important the Almighty viewed the "stand" of Phinehas.

2. Does God see that kind of zeal in your life? How did such a violent act receive such a commendation from God? Only by looking at Phinehas' heart, in context with the circumstances, can one understand how he turned away the wrath of God.

3. Phinehas' act could never be repeated; but his zeal is critically needed today.

a. This point brings us to the emphasis of this dramatic example, which is: YOU, and you alone, have the power to act against the things that curse your own progress with God.

b. Rise up and "stand" against the compromises for sin you see. Remove your foot from the tents of the Moabites. When a false sense of personal exception tempts you to believe you are immune to God's judgment and you can remain silent without being equally damned, rip that callous part from your heart and confront the compromise that is tempting you to join in "peace" with God's enemies (2 Chronicles 19:2; Ezekiel 13:22; 2 Kings 3:13, 14; 1 Kings 22:49).

God has placed His Spirit of righteousness within you; and with it, the power to act in behalf of your own soul (Colossians 3:5; Romans 8:13).

III. "Stand" in the Lord—*Its practicality*

125

A. 🖰 *Taking a "stand" refers to a decision* (Ephesians 6:14, aorist participle). To "stand" in verse 13 denotes the end of the conflict—they chose to take a "stand" in the past (at the beginning of their Christian life). And that choice is spoken of as starting at the beginning but continuing until the end! It is not simply integrity or sincerity that enables this; but it is the assured conviction that one knows and believes God's Truth!

B. 🖰 *Taking a "stand" will enroll you in the list* of those who are chronicled in history's museum of memorable Believers in the Family of the Almighty God.

   1. The person of Phinehas is used throughout Scripture to encourage God's People to "stand" for the divine will.

   2. The prophet Malachi needed to confront a priesthood that had gone wrong. The prophet reached back into Israelite history and turned to Numbers 22-25 and utilized Phinehas. The corruption of the priests in Malachi's day stood in sharp contrast to the devotion of Phinehas. Malachi 2:5b-6 lists the admirable traits of Phinehas which had been forgotten. Malachi bluntly said that the failure of God's People and Priests to emulate the devotion of Phinehas assured the wrathful condemnation of the Almighty God.

C. 🖰 *Taking a "stand" will permit* you to read the blessed words of Psalm 106:30, 31 in a most personal way.

D. 🖰 *Taking a "stand" will bring* a commendation from Almighty God IF you are using Truth as the foundation (Ephesians 6:14)

Conclusion

I. The church of Christ is described in the Epistle to the Ephesians as the glorious Body designed by God. The members of the church of Christ are beneficiaries to all spiritual blessings in the heavenly places. 🖰 God has blessed mankind with His Church, but that blessing brings the immediate attention and attack of Satan.

A. Being a Christian involves living as light and salt—one has to make an impact; silence is not optional. Weeping and wringing one's hands in the face of sin is not sufficient.

B. Christians must STAND—heroically stand; stand with their backs against the wall. There is no other option.

C. Will you emulate Phinehas and stand for the Lord and His Cause even if all around you are willing to be at peace with sin and complacent in righteous zeal?

II. ✋ "Finally, be strong in the Lord, and in the strength (power) of His might" (Ephesians 6:10).

A. Please note the triple reference to the sustaining force available to Christian who "stand"—"strong," "strength (power)," and "might." The one who follows God and STANDS firm in his faith will never run out of energy.

B. King Asa is an excellent illustration (2 Chronicles 14:9-12)—without equal number, without equal military might, and without visible strength...yet he proved to be superior because of his faith and confidence in the Lord God Almighty. Asa stood strong in the Lord and in the strength (power) of His might!

III. *Americans have a national colloquialism which is frequently used when signing documents. This common practice of asking for a person's "John Hancock" comes from the most obvious signature on our Declaration of Independence. John Hancock's name is the only signature that can be easily identified by the casual observer...and that is exactly what he intended. The Declaration was approved on July 4, but it was not signed until August 2. After its initial approval, Jefferson's words were hand printed on parchment in preparation for being sent to the king. This gave Hancock nearly a month to contemplate his actions in signing. As president of the Congress, he felt responsible to make a clear statement to not only the king, but to his fellow countrymen as well. Consequently, he was the first to sign, and as all Americans know, he artistically scrawled his name in large, flowing letters. His expressed intent was to make certain King George III could read his*

127

name without the aid of glasses. It was a bold declaration of his personal commitment to the cause for which he was willing to die. John Hancock's overly legible signature hit the target at which he aimed. During the Revolutionary War, King George offered amnesty to all of the Americans who were willing to stop the war. Hancock and a few select others were intentionally omitted from this proposition. His zealous signature informed the king there was no turning back, and the British Empire clearly heard that strong message of commitment. All of us have been asked to give our "John Hancock" in a variety of settings. Among those settings should be our loyalty to keeping the local Church pure and exactly as God designed it to be—the haven for His spiritual Family. Fifty-six delegates signed the Declaration of Independence, but only one name stands out above the others because John Hancock wanted the king to know where he stood with his country. Has your signature let the King of Kings know where you stand with His church? (Houston Chronicle, 1998).

See Psalm 112:1; 119:97ff.

12-26

- 11 -

The Character and Cunning
of the Destructionist

Introduction

I. The term "destructionist" is rarely used in the common language. Yet, it identifies the focus of this study. By definition it refers to "one who delights in destroying that which is valuable, or whose principles and influence tend to destroy existing institutions; an advocate of the destruction of an existing political institution or the like." Thus, the focus is upon a person who is determined to "deconstruct" the existing framework that sets boundaries for acceptable and unacceptable behavior and beliefs.

The world has always been tempted by the cunning Destructionist who attempts to "change" or "rethink" or "redefine" issues. Their objective is to "deconstruct" the old and "reconstruct" the new. They display an arrogant anarchy.

The root of all specific evils found in this world is anarchy—the rejection of the rule of law for civility. An observation of all the evil events and characters that have blackened the history of civilization reveals that anarchy was the governing impetus. Beginning with the Satan's temptation of Eve and progressing to the current disruption of civility in our world, all is focused on rejecting what God says by supplanting what man wants. This is illustrated clearly by Eve's rejection of God's rule for anarchy's governing, "(T)he woman saw that the tree was good for food, and that it was a delight to the eyes, and that the tree was desirable to make one wise, she took from its fruit and ate; and she gave also to her husband with her, and he ate" (Genesis 3:6).

Eve decided to govern her choices and behavior on what she "saw," on what she "thought" would result, on what she "desired" for self, and to obtain what she wanted with the least work and effort on her part. She wanted to be "wise."

II.   Such is the undisputable analysis of anarchy—it urges people to cast aside God's Rule and follow the deceptive promises of self-satisfaction. The problem with anarchy is that it *never* works. It *never* satisfies. It *never* brings happiness. It always brings ruin.

1-2

Body

I.   Anarchy's Historic Secular Illustration

A study of the dark pages of civilization repeatedly illustrates the despair of anarchy. Whether it is the savagery of Attila, or the Mongol Khans, or the barbarism of the pagan Nordic hordes, the conclusion is the same—lawlessness brings disastrous consequences. There is no way to offer a revisionist's commentary that can applaud the evils of anarchy.

The unimpeachable Truth firmly remains—in order for mankind to enjoy life, so as to find peace and blessings and happiness and success, man MUST follow a system of Law that governs belief systems and conduct. Within society there MUST be clarity in distinguishing what is right and what is wrong. As long as those in society submit to the Rule of Law, then all is good. A failure to submit brings catastrophe.

This point is illustrated by what historians call "The Terror" that resulted from the French Revolution. In that dark historical context, the rise of anarchy resulted in a total repudiation of the Rule of Law. The practice of anarchy was common on the most basic levels of daily life. That rejection of the Rule of Law and the governing by anarchy has accurately been described as "The Terror."

One has made this astute analysis of the development leading to "The Terror." *"It is ironic that of all countries in Europe, France was the only one that could have had a revolution—not because she groaned under the lash of tyranny, but, on the contrary, because she tolerated and even invited every conceivable dissension and heresy. Restlessness, a passion for novelty and the pursuit of excitement were everywhere in the air. They were the fruits of idleness and leisure, not of poverty"* (Lomis, 11-12).

Did you notice that the initiating cause of this evil period was the rejection of an absolute Rule of Law and the acceptance of the spirit of anarchy that Eve's sin revealed? Anarchy cast aside rules and followed "every conceivable dissension and heresy." The general population was encouraged to live with "restlessness, a passion for novelty and the pursuit of excitement." The general public was urged to reject completely the Rule of Law that had guarded civility.

The French Revolution is not the only instance of this evil. It is one of the clearest illustrations; but, tragically, it is not unique in civilization. As shown from the Garden account, anarchy has tempted and damned mankind "from the beginning." History reveals that through the centuries anarchy has changed its vocabulary of enticing words to persuade unthinking man to follow its illusions.

Anarchy clearly appears when one is looking retrospectively at its terror and ruin. It is unbelievable how some are so blind to anarchy's illusions that they are caught in its snare. It is sobering to realize that eventually all following anarchy will be exposed as instigators of lawlessness and their evil influence will continue to bring lawlessness to society. (A good illustration of this point is King Manasseh who ruled Judah with an anarchist's agenda. Ultimately he came to see his evil and repented, but his pattern of anarchy continued to damn those he influenced—2 Kings 21:1-17; 2 Chronicles 33:10-17.)

A contemporary illustration of the delusion of anarchy is found in the words of the elected leader of the world's greatest super-powers. The comment says, "I have done what I thought best for this nation" (January 20, 2015). Notice that his governing principle was not the nation's Rule of Law (The Constitution he had sworn to uphold) BUT it was "what I thought best." No other phrase frighteningly summarizes the disdain for the absolute Rule of Law.

Anarchy's evil leaven compromises all aspects of civilization. Perhaps the anarchy in civil matters is identified as the most frequent form of the lawless attitude. But anarchy's abhorrence of rules is seen in every aspect of civilization (the home, governments, and religion).

The greatest tragedy that can befall a nation and drive it into total anarchy occurs when the Laws of the nation are mocked and citizens are told they can, with impunity, disobey a Law which they do not like.

Many are duped into rejecting the rule of order in their private lives thinking that what they do is "nobody's business." Consequently, "personal choice" becomes the governing rule and mockingly ignores all other standards. This form of anarchy has developed the governing anarchy of "tolerance" in our society.

Anarchy has historically compromised religious beliefs and practices. Ever since the Satan deceived Adam and Eve in the Garden, man has often followed his own governing in religious faith and practices. I have often heard people say, "I know what God's Word (the Bible) says BUT I think God is going to look at matters differently." Even a casual reading of the Scriptures provides multiple illustrations of this fact. Man is cautioned not to allow the deceptive governing of anarchy to direct him (Jeremiah 10:23; see Jeremiah 6:13-17 for a heartbreaking anecdote of this cancerous evil).

The greatest tragedy that can befall God's Church and drive it into total anarchy occurs when the Laws of God are mocked and Christians are told they can, with impunity, disobey a commanded practice or modify a faith principle which they do not like.

A contemporary illustration of the delusion of anarchy is seen in the words of some elderships who confess "We have done what we thought best for this congregation to grow." But notice that their governing principle is not the Scripture's Rule of Law (The Bible) BUT it was "what we think is best to make this congregation to grow."

No other phrase frighteningly summarizes the disdain modern religious leaders have for the absolute spiritual Rule of Law.

II. Anarchy's Devilish Spiritual Deconstruction

The two epistles to the Thessalonica Church are encouraging studies. The Church began in the midst of persecution. Paul was able to remain there only three weeks before fleeing for his life because of anarchy (Acts 17:1-9). But after Paul's departure, the Thessalonica brethren demonstrated a tenacious devotion to God (1 Thessalonians 2:12-14).

The Second Coming of Christ and the resurrection were repeated points in 1 Thessalonians that offered the beleaguered brethren sustaining hope (the Second Coming is mentioned in every chapter of 1 Thessalonians). These doctrines emphasized that this troubled world is not our destiny—we are only passing through and ultimately will find eternal peace in heaven. This hope sustained the brethren and guarded their hearts.

Not long after he wrote the first epistle, the Apostle Paul sent the second epistle. Second Thessalonians contains only three brief chapters. The second epistle stresses two basic points to encourage Christians whose hope was wavering. Once again Paul focuses upon the Second Coming and then issues a strong caution regarding false doctrine.

The Church at Thessalonica remained faithful in spite of constant persecution (2 Thessalonians 1:3, 4). But it appears that some had infected the congregation with false doctrine that would degrade the hope that guarded their spiritual security.

Some had arisen in the congregation and advocated a gross misunderstanding about the Lord's Second Coming. This false teaching had led to questioning God's promises (2 Thessalonians 2:1, 2). This false teaching had so affected the congregation that some lost all hope and, consequently, stopped working. They still attended the congregation and had interaction with the members, but they were idle busybodies further weakening the congregation (2 Thessalonians 3:11, 12).

As Inspiration addresses this situation, Paul uses each of the three chapters to stress a single point that when combined present an encouraging lesson for the saints. He commends them for their steadfastness and faith (chapter 1) and then shows how their commendable faith should have protected them from false teaching (chapter 2). He then concludes by urging them to act by faith and correct the error and not give up their faith and reputation (chapter 3).

Here is a message of hope that stresses how security and blessings result when Christians follow God's absolute Laws.

The Church in Thessalonians had suffered persecution from its beginning. They had witnessed Paul's persecution but had been encouraged by his trust in God's Word. They imitated his allegiance and stood fast even though beset by persecution. They were able to persevere because they were trusting in the hope of the Lord's return (2 Thessalonians 1:4). But now someone had "troubled" them with false reports about "the day of the Lord." This denied them the security of their "hope."

The point for our study is this—only by trusting, obeying, and enforcing God's absolute Laws can one find a solid faith in a turbulent world.

III. Anarchy's Devious Work

Paul's words detail how the brethren in Thessalonica were attacked by anarchy's evil.

Anarchy exists when there is a deliberate rejection of the absolute Rule of Law. As long as the governing Law remains enforced, civility will result and allegiance to order will be maintained. However, once the governing Rule of Law is first questioned and then suspected, the Anarchist (Destructionist) finds opportunity to sow his evil rebellion.

This process is well illustrated throughout Scripture. One of the clearest instances is found in the failed attempt of the anarchists Korah, Dathan and Abiram as they sought to wrest the Rule of Law away from Moses and Aaron in Numbers 16:1-35. They planted evil questions regarding God's Law. They stimulated the suspicions that they had aroused and stirred rebellion. It is sadly amusing to note that these anarchists accused Moses and Aaron of taking too much authority (16:3) and yet they were seizing the arrogant authority to overthrow God's Rule of Law.

Those seeking to rethink and redefine God's Rule of Law today would do well to read again Numbers 16:1-35 and review the damnable destiny ahead for all who try to supplant God's Rule of Law!

How did anarchy attempt to supplant God's Rule of Law in Thessalonica? Their cunning scheme is exposed in 2 Thessalonians 2:2. They sought to replace the clear teaching of Inspiration with counterfeit truth. Some reported that Paul "said" the Second Coming was already past. Others claimed to produce a pseudo-epistle from Paul claiming the Second Coming was history. Paul's blunt response declared such "coming is in accord with the activity of Satan."

The devilish Destructionists utilized emotional appeals. The deceived brethren were led to trust in emotions and not the absolute Truth of God (2 Thessalonians 2:7-12). And the inevitable end is that those thus deceived are damned "because they did not receive the love of the truth so as to be saved (but followed) a deluding influence so that they will believe what is false, in order that they all may be judged (because they) did not believe the truth, but took pleasure in wickedness."

Anarchy presents a tragic irony. It seeks to do away with all Law. It strives to promote absolute freedom. It condemns any exclusive boundaries. Yet, the Anarchist enforces his own Rule of Law! The real intent of the Anarchist is to deny God's order and to promote Self's order. This is the only objective and it wholly focused upon SELF. It is relentless in satisfying Self. It is merciless and intolerant of anyone who does not applaud his arrogance.

Anarchy is not a Rule of Law to govern a population with civility, but it is a Rule of Law that is based on selfishness. It presents a façade of justice but it is pure evil contrived by a self-serving arrogance (again review the "Reign of Terror" in France to see a somber illustration of this fact).

In order to accomplish its dastardly result, anarchy must cause the governing Rule of Law to be first questioned, then suspected of error and finally to be discarded as a "past" event. This operational principle is true as anarchy seeks to destroy national governments. It is also tragically true as anarchy seeks to destroy God's spiritual governing.

This is why God repeatedly urges His followers to maintain Truth, teach Truth, uphold Truth, and defend the Truth. When people are ignorant of God's Truth, they are ruled by anarchy and destruction soon follows (see this situation addressed by Hosea 4:1-7).

How disconcerting it is to see God's People refuse to know God's Word and think they can escape the consequences.

IV. Anarchy's EVIL Spiritual Results

The results of anarchy are pure evil. There is nothing good about abandoning the absolute Rule of Law to allow the gratification of self-centered desires. This point is clear in any governing context (national, personal, spiritual).

Let us focus on the evils that result when anarchy usurps God's absolute Truth in spiritual matters of belief and behavior.

A. *First*, the attack strategy of anarchy targets the confidence of Christians and strives to cause them to be "shaken" in their convictions. The word "shaken" is from the Greek term σαλεύω and means "to waver, to be agitated or rocked so that the object shaken is toppled or destroyed." It refers to an object being moved from a former position. It can also refer to *a* "stirring up" of a previously stable environment.

The Thessalonian brethren had found stability and confidence in the words of Inspiration. But now false teachers had injected questions and suspicions and the blessed stability was missing. This resulted from teaching that was not based upon the Bible. The stability that brings blessings is not from one's "thoughts" or "how do you feel this applies," but from clear teaching about the behavior and belief that God's absolute Truth commands—a direct "thus saith the Lord!"

Once one leaves the absolute commands of God, he becomes unstable. To the Ephesians Paul would liken such to a piece of driftwood that is tossed about in any direction (Ephesians 4:14, 15).

When a congregation no longer adheres to the absolute Truth of God in matters of doctrine and practice they have been "shaken" and such instability brings only greater problems.

B. *Second*, the effectiveness of anarchy requires that the Rule of Law be "soon" replaced by the rule of self-willed arrogance. The word "soon" can also be translated as "easily." It comes from the Greek term ταχέως and refers to a sequence of time. The action that it describes occurs speedily or rapidly. Such occurs because those involved act hastily. Those in a congregation affected by the Destructionist (Anarchist/Change Agent) are dazed at the chaos and the dramatic changes that mark their worship and practices. They shake their heads saying, "How did this happen so quickly?"

The situation described by this adverb occurs because a hasty response was made. In the context of 2 Thessalonians, the hasty action was the "shaking" of the brethren's confidence in God's Truth. They lost the firm assurance because they quickly forgot the Truth that Paul had taught. Thus, Paul chided them by saying, "Do you not remember that while I was still with you, I was telling you these things?" (2:5).

When a congregation quickly accepts the redefined doctrines or the "revisited" practices of the New Testament Church, they are following the same mistake that the brethren in Thessalonica did. God's Truth never changes. But the Anarchist must persuade Christians that Truth can change and that they must do it quickly.

Once the Anarchist's propositions and his new-found understanding is measured by a study of God's Word, it will be exposed as false. So the Anarchist must persuade his targeted victims to act hastily and without study of the Scriptures.

It is critical for the Christian to remember that anarchist changes (repudiation of the governing Law) in one's culture provide the foundation for anarchist changes in the Church! Once culture has lost the war with anarchy and the absolute Rule of Law ceases to govern secular civility, then it will only be a brief time before anarchy invades and destroys the spiritual Rule of Law. This is why Paul urges us, "And do not be conformed to this world, but be transformed by the renewing of your mind, so that you may prove what the will of God is, that which is good and acceptable and perfect" (Romans 12:2).

C. **Third**, the method of anarchy is to cause Christians to be "troubled." The term "troubled" comes from the Greek word θροέω, throeo͞, and refers to a deep mourning of one's spirit. It causes him to wail or clamor in distress at what is going on in life. It refers to a fear caused by insecurity. One thus allows fear to control life so that faith is overruled; excited efforts are made to quiet the fear that is causing the distress.

In spiritual issues this occurs when Christians are induced to accept a troubling anxiety about the beliefs and practices of the Church. They are led to believe that the "old paths" are leading to futility, lessening numbers, and ultimately a disappearance of the Church! So fear (troubling) causes decisions to be made to trust upon man's worldly wisdom and not upon God's revelation. Inspiration's commands are set aside for anarchy's arrogance and modern idolatry emerges.

This is what happened in Thessalonica and Paul immediately addressed this fear. His inspired counsel was simple, "Do not be goaded by fear and think that God's absolute Truth is not applicable to your situation! Do not surrender to troubling times but trust absolutely on God's commands!" (paraphrased by JLK).

Such a message speaks to every congregation of God's People today! Do not surrender the absolutes of faith and practice because you are "troubled" by factors that draw your sight away from God's Truth and onto worldly standards. If today's congregations allow their faith and practice to be "redefined" by anarchy, they will never find comfort in the conviction of God's absolute Truth but instead will discover constant irritants and unsettling personalities (See 2 Peter 2:9-19).

Christians ought not to be "troubled" (to fear; be apprehensive; be anxious) by the Destructionist. Those who seek to turn us away from the absolute Truth of God's Bible cannot provide the comfort that is found in following the absolutes of God's Bible. God's righteousness reigns from the heavenly throne—God is the Almighty Sovereign and presides in all earthly affairs (Habakkuk 2:20). This provides a security that cannot be found in anarchy's deconstruction of biblical belief and behavior.

D. *Fourth*, the tool of anarchy is deception. This is a shocking fact. We have the Holy Scriptures that provide us understanding and insight yet many are quick to follow actions, teachings, and expressions in worship that are contrary to the Scriptures. These are convinced that the "old" must give way to the "new." They openly embrace the Destructionist's agenda and with shocking speed they leave God's Truth for anarchy's arrogance.

Their deception leads to a complete change in belief and practice.

This amazing change is because the Satan has manipulated the surrender of biblical allegiance by "deception." The English word for "deception" is translated by the Greek term ἐξαπατάω and means "to cheat" or "to thoroughly deceive." The thought communicated by this word describes one that is so deceived that he accepts falsehood for the Truth. And he believes error MORE that he believes Truth (See Colossians 2:4, 18). In James 1:22 the word is παραλογίζομαι and means "to miscalculate." It refers to being beguiled by mere probability.

Adding emphasis to this calamity are the somber words with which Inspiration offers a more complete explanation of the doom awaiting those who surrender God's absolute Truth to anarchy's evil arrogance. "Then that lawless one will be revealed whom the Lord will slay with the breath of His mouth and bring to an end by the appearance of His coming; that is, the one whose coming is in accord with the activity of Satan, with all power and signs and false wonders, and with all the deception of wickedness for those who perish, because they did not receive the love of the truth so as to be saved. For this reason God will send upon them a deluding influence so that they will believe what is false, in order that they all may be judged who did not believe the truth, but took pleasure in wickedness." (2 Thessalonians 2:8-12).

The tragedy of the evil spiritual Destructionist is summarized in these few words: They do not LOVE the Truth and thus they will perish!

V. Anarchy ANSWERED And Rejected

Inspiration is never silent regarding how Christian's are to address those seeking to destroy the foundations of God's absolute authority. In addressing the same attack against God's authority in the Church in Crete, Inspiration commanded, "For there are many rebellious men, empty talkers and deceivers, especially those of the circumcision, who must be silenced because they are upsetting whole families, teaching things they should not teach for the sake of sordid gain." (Titus 1:10-11; see also Titus 2:7, 8).

The point to note from Inspiration's directive to Crete is found in the Greek term ἀνυπότακτος (anupotaktos). This refers to "one who is unsubdued, insubordinate, disobedient to the revealed commands and consequently has a self-governing authority (anarchy) that refuses to put self's actions under authority; unruly."

The Scriptures portray mankind involved an unrelenting spiritual war that calls all to become soldiers in either God's army of righteousness or supporters in the Satan's army of destruction.

There is no neutral ground. There is no common ground upon which a ceasefire agreement can be reached so that all can "live in peace."

The Destructionist is governed by the Satan's mandate that requires a total destruction of God's pattern and then a reconstruction of a religious pattern that is far different from what God had commanded. (Note: This conflict is often seen in the myriad of military terms and metaphors that urge Christians to persevere and go forward. Such is indeed an intriguing and rewarding study of the behavior and actions required from God's People, but we do not have the space or thesis for it in this paper. However, we will reference a few of these and urge readers to explore this point further in their own study).

Paul writes to the brethren in Thessalonica who were confronted with anarchy's efforts to destroy God's commanded belief and behavior, and urges them to confront the efforts of the Destructionist. Three points immediately arise:

First, Christians must maintain fidelity to the absoluteness of God's revealed Truth. This attacks the most critical foundation of belief and practice. God's revealed truth (the Bible) is the governing authority that commands belief and practices that please the Almighty God. As long as one follows this governing standard then God will be pleased. However, it is this governing authority that the Destructionist seeks to discredit and replace with his anarchist's agenda.

This challenge is well illustrated by John 18:38. Pilate asked the question that anticipated the cultural situation in our day—"What is Truth?" Many really believe there is no absolute Truth; all is relative and depends upon feelings. This prevailing philosophy in modern culture is generally accepted. All have come to believe that "it does not matter what one believes as long as they are sincere and loving."

Amazingly, this philosophical outlook is evidenced in every aspect of modern culture. Today's culture is allowed to dictate and approve actions that are blatantly contrary to what the Scriptures teach. This philosophy is evidenced in politics, diplomacy, business ventures, personal choices, legal courts AND religious practices. Many will admit there is a disconnect between what the Bible teaches and what religious people profess and practice. Why have things changed? Because of the same reason the Thessalonians were being "quickly shaken"—today's religious confidence is not based upon God's Word but upon a Selfish idolatry (See Exodus 32:8).

How does true Science validate natural truth? It is not upon the personal whims and feelings of the individual, but upon the tried and repeated testing that results in the same conclusions. This same process is the only way to validate spiritual Truth. God has given us an absolute criterion by which spiritual judgment is confidently based.

Today people thoughtlessly repudiate the old standards. Once Truth is discounted or redefined, catastrophic events will come (see Hosea 4:1-6 for a description of the practical reality of a society that refuses to follow God's revealed word).

Notice the following words that Inspiration deliberately chose to tell Christians how they must confront the anarchy of the Destructionist.

A. **"Stand fast"** (2:15) comes from the Greek term στήκω (stekō) and communicates the idea that one remains stationary or perseveres. That action leads one to stand firm in faith and duty. This is used in an absolute sense and means there is no acceptable reason for one NOT to do this.

B. **"Hold"** (2:15) comes from the Greek term κρατέω (krateō). This word communicates the idea that one is using great strength (a strenuous effort) to seize or retain or keep, obtain, retain, or take by strength. This describes an aggressive energy (See 2 Timothy 1:13). The Christian is NOT congratulated on his ability to find common ground or to appease those opposed to God's absolute standard, but is commended for holding the Truth in an uncompromised way.

This term means the Christian is to show a strong loyalty to the revealed commands of God in belief and practice. When it comes to the Bible, one must be in complete control; one must be the master because of an understanding of its precepts. One is not to allow the lessening of the Scriptures in its governing. One must seize, cleave to, strictly observe and guard the Holy Scriptures in belief and behavior.

C. **"Traditions"** (2:15) is a despised term for the Anarchist. The bitter rejection of God's traditions comes because the Destructionist must repudiate the basic governing of beliefs and behavior in order to reconstruct the "new" governing order. Thus, the Destructionist assumes the role of a "Change Agent" as he seeks to deceive and change God's commands.

The word "traditions" is from the Greek term παράδοσις (paradosis) and refers to a process of transmission of a precept, ordinance, or practice.

God's Truth rests upon "traditions" (2:15). God's Church is commanded to follow "traditions." We cannot discount this by using absurdities that have evolved in the religious community and generalize saying "all traditionalism is wrong" (2 Thessalonians 2:15; 3:6; Titus 2:7).

The Bible is very clear on this point—2 Thessalonians 2:15 "So then, brethren, stand firm and hold to the traditions which you were taught, whether by word of mouth or by letter from us." Also pay close attention to this verse, "(I)n all things show yourself to be an example [i.e. pattern] of good deeds, with purity in doctrine, dignified" (Titus 2:7).

Inspiration's emphatic reminder to struggling saints is to find security in the divine absolutes—"the traditions" taught by Inspiration, NOT the pleasing rhetoric of worldly minds (1 Corinthians 2:1ff).

Note: There are "traditions of men" that are contrary to God's Law (see Matthew 15:9; Mark 7:7). The Destructionist mocks the traditions of God by placing the divinely commanded traditions on the same level as the absurd traditions of man. Their evil is magnified as they reduced the sovereignty of the Almighty God to the absurdities of man's ignorance. How frightening it is to contemplate the Divine wrath one will face because he rejected God's traditions and he urged others to reject the commanded beliefs and practices with mocking scorn and contempt for the holy! Such is inexcusable and should be instantly challenged and never coddled!

D. **"Taught"** (2:15)–this term references the fact that God's commands (traditions) must be communicated! God's People are an educated people. Faith is founded upon knowledge that provides an absolute assurance (1 John 5:13).

A failure to teach always results in a failed society. The Dark Ages were the natural consequent to the ignorance that controlled the population. The historic apostasy of the Church resulted because of the failure of man to know God's Word. God's People are always a people of education—they stress learning; they begin schools; they focus on "knowing" the revealed Truth; they "know the Book."

"By word or Epistle" (2:15) validates the fact that God's governing authority rests upon the process of Inspiration. God's Truth was revealed by inspired communications that were committed to writing. The written Word becomes the absolute governing authority in religious belief and behavior. If mankind wishes to enjoy a civility that proves peace, security, and personal joy, he must follow the written Word as the absolute governing in every aspect of society.

E. **"Pattern"** (Titus 2:7) is a word that elicits the greatest vehemence from the Destructionist. It is the "pattern" of God that the Anarchist loathes. The Destructionist/Change Agent cannot say enough to deride "pattern theology." Regardless of what the raging enemy of God's governing pattern may say, he

We sing acapella because of The Tradition ~~...~~ because God commanded it cannot deny the Truth that God has provided mankind with a "pattern" of what to believe and practice!

The term "pattern" is from the Greek word τύπος (tupos) and refers specifically to a form that is to be followed. It is used to communicate a die or a stamp by which replication is to be made. (Can you imagine one who would say that those manufacturing parts for a car's engine do not have to cast the parts according to the die? And yet the Destructionist has convinced many that one does not have to follow the die that God has provided for His Church!) The term "pattern" is also used in reference to one replicating a shape, a statue, a style or resemblance. Specifically it is used to describe a model that is an imitation.

God's governing expects man to follow God's directives. He has provided us the model; He has given us the shape and style to replicate. It is God's blueprint for what HE desires and He expects us to follow the directives without any modification (Revelation 22:18, 19; see these illustrations of what God expects from those who have His pattern in Genesis 6:22; 7:9b; Exodus 25:40; 31:11b; 34:11; 39:5, 7, 21, 26, 29, 31, 32, 42, 43; 40:16-32).

The Christian should strive for his service to be presented to God as was Israel's after they constructed the Tabernacle. "And Moses examined all the work and behold, they had done it; just as the Lord had commanded, this they had done. So Moses blessed them" (Exodus 39:43).

Second, Christians must maintain faithfulness to our pledged allegiance. When one confesses Christ as the Son of God as commanded by God, that is a statement of allegiance (Matthew 10:32 33). A failure to maintain that pledged allegiance is an act of treason and must be treated as a heinous act.

There are two specific areas where Christians must maintain a faithful loyalty to God's plan. These areas are often attacked by those seeking to change God's order with their destructionist agenda.

First, we must maintain faithfulness to the Word of God. Paul's concern for the Thessalonian brethren is simply stated, "So then, brethren, stand fast, and hold the traditions which ye were taught, whether by word, or by epistle of ours" (2 Thessalonians 2:15, ASV). The Apostle's point was that the Church will only maintain its allegiance IF it follows the revealed directives of God. These are taught by the Inspired verbal Word and Inspired written Epistles.

This same emphasis is found in Titus 1:9 where the Greek term ἀντέχομαι (antechomai) is used. There Inspiration states, "(H)olding to the faithful word which is according to the teaching, that he may be able to exhort in the sound doctrine, and to convict the gainsayers." Inspiration chose to use a word that stresses Christians are to be opposite from others who contradict and deny God's governing commands for belief and behavior. In contrast to those who mock and treat with contempt the commands and practices of God, the Christian is to adhere to, care for, and support the "faithful Word of God."

Second, there must be faithfulness to the commanded order. This explains HOW Christians maintain faithfulness to the Word of God. One faithfully holds to the Word of God by maintaining the order that God commands for His Church.

An emphatic verse for this study is 2 Thessalonians 3:6 "Now we command you, brethren, in the name of our Lord Jesus Christ, that ye withdraw yourselves from every brother that walketh disorderly, and not after the tradition which they received of us" (ASV).

There is a definite "order"—one can either be "orderly" or be "disorderly." Proper order is essential and expected from those who are following God (1 Timothy 3:15).

The term "disorderly" is from the Greek word ἀτάκτως (ataktōs) and refers to action that is disorderly or insubordinate to the governing commands. It is taught that those who are not living according to the apostolic traditions are NOT obeying God. Their lives do NOT reflect submission to God but a rebellion against God. Used in 1 Thessalonians 5:14, it refers to the insubordinate—the one "out of step" with the teachings of God.

"To violate the rules (of Inspiration's traditions) is to 'walk disorderly'—to break the ranks; to fall out of line. The value of the individual soldier is the degree in which he keeps in order and acts in perfect harmony and precision with the rest of the

regiment. A breach of military rule creates disaster. Let the believer keep the Law and the Law will keep him" (Excell, 576).

The idea communicated by this term is that one demonstrates an irregularity with the known standards. This term defines "disorderly conduct." How is one's conduct "disorderly"? They are "disorderly" when their actions and expressions are irregular with the prevailing law. The same point applies to one's religious beliefs and practices—they are "disorderly" when their beliefs, actions and expressions are irregular with the revealed will of God taught either by Word or Epistle!

Note: The practicality for this "order" in the Lord's Church is essential because the Church is in a war and a failure of any army to maintain order results in its quick destruction. Thus, each Christian is expected to walk in step with the traditions that were delivered by Inspiration—these are our marching orders! Any stepping out of order must be addressed or he will be lost and possibly be the cause of other's defeat (Galatians 6:1-2; 1 Corinthians 5:1-6).

"If all efforts to recover the recalcitrant fail, then the Church has the highest authority for separating completely from the society and fellowship of such. Continued communion with them would not only seem to condone their offence, but destroy discipline, and put an end to all moral consistency" (Exell, 576).

This order is based not upon man's fickle feelings, but upon the sovereign rule of the Almighty God.

The term "Command" or "Charge" has a military sense to it. It references an order issued by the Commander to the troops. And this order must be obeyed. It comes from the Greek term παραγγέλλω (paraggellō) and refers to transmitting a message that enjoins, charges, commands or declares (See 1 Timothy 1:18). The stress of this word is upon an absolute authority...there is no redefining the "commands." Inspiration chided those who were quickly shaken by saying, "You have been taught...and the teaching has not changed!" (paraphrased by JLK).

The word "Order" is also a military term referencing the command and control that is essential for an army to be victorious. The stress of this word is that each is to "walk in step" and remain "in line" with the Commander's orders so the unit will not fall into disarray and be defeated.

Those following God's governing will maintain the proper order by following the same commands. Those not following God's governing will destroy the orderly and demonstrate disorder (which is the consequence of anarchy).

The use of the term "walketh disorderly" (2 Thessalonians 3:6) is translated from the Greek term ἀτάκτως (ataktos). This adverb describes an immoral irregularity that has caused a disruption of the previous order. The Destructionists are not content to submit to God's commands in belief and practice. They arrogantly walk "out of step" with God's revealed Word. Their practice is described as a continuous rejection (being constantly out of rank and file) with God's Word. Their behavior is a stubborn practice that will not change. "Walketh" is a present participle indicating constant action. Thus, the tragic observation, some are intent on following constantly a religious pattern that is not approved of God.

Another text that corroborates Paul's counsel to the Thessalonian Church is found in Titus 1:10 where the English term "unruly" is translated from the Greek word ἀνυπότακτος (anupotaktos). This word is used to describe one who is unsubdued by authority. He is insubordinate or disobedient and is not content to put himself under authority. He is unruly.

Third, Christians must maintain a fellowship that is intolerant of the Destructionist's agenda. In order for a fighting force to find victory, there must be a trusting, cohesive camaraderie that performs in an orderly fashion. In the Lord's Church this is described as "fellowship." In order for the Lord's Army to be victorious, there must be a cohesive uncompromised fellowship.

The Destructionist recognizes this critical fact so his priority is to compromise the exclusive fellowship of God. By doing away with the definition of fellowship that God's Word provides, the Destructionist redefines fellowship terms and thereby establishes boundaries that are condemned by God's authority (see 2 Corinthians 6:14-18 for a discussion of this point).

For those seeking to deconstruct New Testament Christianity, the issue of fellowship must be "deconstructed" and then "reconstructed" in the anarchist's perception. The Deconstructionist has accepted the false premise that absolute Truth is deniable and that practical Truth is a matter of personal choice and depends on each situation. Consequently, there are no firm behaviorisms expected. Each is allowed to do whatever he chooses (Judges 17:6) and there are no immoral behaviors.

The Deconstructionist (a.k.a. Spiritual Anarchist; Change Agent) denies there is no way one can walk disorderly or be insubordinate or be subversive to God's will as long as he is sincere and following some contorted understanding of "love." Today's emphasis is that sincerity and "love" is the only governing criteria. And...anarchy has triumphed over steadfast fidelity to God's Word!

Consequently, the Church has been compromised. And a compromised Church becomes WORSE than members in a pagan group (1 Corinthians 5:1; 2 Peter 2:20-22). An astute observation notes four facts about the disorderly in the Church.

1. *The disorderly in the Church violate the rules that give compactness and strength to all Church organization.*

2. *The disorderly in the Church ignore the highest examples of moral consistency.*

3. *The disorderly in the Church should be faithfully warned and counseled.*

4. *The disorderly in the Church, if incorrigible, should be excluded from the privilege of Christian fellowship.* (Excell, 577)

VI. Anarchy's Evil Threat To Modern Christians

The Thessalonica brethren faced a dire situation...relatively babes in Christ they were being pulled away from God's Truth by those seeking to supplant the governing authority of God's Scriptures. Consequently, doubt was planted; discouragement was present; disillusionment with their eternal hope (resurrection) was evident. As a result of God's authority being questioned the congregation faced these perils—instability in faith issues and insecurity in their doctrinal beliefs. Paul addressed these issues so the Church would be pulled back from the disastrous ruin approaching.

Second Thessalonians is a marvelous study with very practical meaning for today's Church. It emphasizes the urgency of submitting to God's authority in our beliefs and behavior!

Two practical results arise when God's holy doctrines that regulate belief and behavior are destroyed by the Deconstructionist.

First, the Destructionist discourages work in the Church (3:13). It is commonly suggested that some had stopped working because they were awaiting the Second Coming. From the context, in which the Christians were discouraged by those claiming that the Second Coming was already past, it would be reasonable to see that those quit because they had lost all hope; they were totally discouraged. The Second Coming had been the basis for their perseverance under trials. But now they faced the false teachers who said this hope was gone. So they just quit. Instead of being productive members in the congregation they were siphoning the energy and resources. Paul urged them to remember how he (Timothy and Silas) behaved when confronted with discouraging actions; they continued to be active and loyal to God!

When the true beliefs and behaviors commanded by God are denied, those who had hope in such are disheartened. False doctrine never edifies. It always destroys.

Those seeking to deconstruct the absolute Truth of the Bible will attack and destroy the basic foundations of belief and behavior. A look at the "liberal" or "progressive" churches validates this fact—such are populated by the "takers" and not the "givers." When a financial need for preaching the gospel's doctrine arises, it will NOT be funded by those clamoring for change. The Destructionists never donate the money and sacrifice the energy to help the Church fulfill its obligation. Pure anarchy does not care for others because it looks only at self!

An amazing fact is observed in congregations where the Deconstructionists (Change Agents; Anarchists) are at work. Often the elders listen to the malcontents and change the belief and behavior of the congregation thinking that such a change will yield more workers, greater attendance, and increased giving. But such does not ever happen because the character of the Deconstructionist (Change Agent; Anarchist) does not care for the standards of the "old" system. They accept these small, incremental changes and continue to press for the complete deconstruction they seek. When the elders agree to these initial "small" changes, it only whets the appetite of anarchy!

Compromise is never satisfied with "common ground." A common ploy of the Anarchist is to present himself as seeking common ground (beliefs and behaviors) upon which all can agree. The Anarchist claims that the objections to distinctive beliefs and behavior are legitimate. He claims that distinctive beliefs and behaviors are divisive. The clamor is then made that if the distinctive beliefs and behaviors are silenced then "peace and love" will reign. All is phrased to grant legitimacy to these self-willed desires. So the Anarchist presents himself as innocent and seeking "common ground" and those refusing to allow the deconstruction of the beliefs and behaviors are "ignorant legalists."

This reminds me of a fable I heard a long time ago. It told of a hunter seeking to kill a bear because the hunter wanted a fur coat. The hunter came upon a bear and was about to shoot it when the bear said, "What are you doing?" The hunter said, "I want a fur coat." The bear replied, "Well I'm hungry and I want a full belly." After further discussion the bear said, "I think I have the answer to our situation and both of us can get what he wants (the bear was offering the hunter "common ground"). The hunter agreed to listen to the bear. And then only the bear was presented at the end as he was sitting by the camp fire the hunter had built. The bear was enjoying his full stomach and the hunter was inside a warm fur coat!

Compromise is NEVER an option for God's Church! Compromise is capitulation! Carefully notice the words of Joshua as he urged Israel to remain firm against the enticements of compromise (Joshua 24:13-24). The significant term in this great address is the phrase "but we will serve the Lord" (verse 15). The word "serve" refers to work that is done by one "enslaved" to another.

The basic idea is that the servant has no authority to change his service--no change to any extent. The servant is to execute the Master's directives without modification. Israel had a choice as to whom they would "serve" (be enslaved to). They could be enslaved to the ungodly idols of paganism or they could be enslaved to their own desires or they could be enslaved to the Lord God Almighty. Joshua's family was very clear. They would be enslaved ONLY to the Lord God Jehovah! No compromise. No seeking "common ground."

Second, the Destructionist faces God's fury (1:7-9). 2 Peter 2:9-19 (ASV) offers one of the most terrifying verdicts upon those who are "self-willed and daring" (the Anarchist, Deconstructionist; Change Agent). "The Lord knoweth how...to keep the unrighteous under punishment unto the day of judgment...Daring, self-willed, they tremble not to rail at dignities...these, as creatures without reason, born mere animals to be taken and destroyed, railing in matters whereof they are ignorant, shall in their destroying surely be destroyed...spots and blemishes, reveling in their deceivings while they feast with you...enticing unstedfast souls; having a heart exercised in covetousness; children of cursing; forsaking the right way, they went astray...uttering great swelling words of vanity, they entice...promising them liberty, while they themselves are bondservants of corruption."

Conclusion

Today's Church lives in a culture that is rabidly anti-Christian. We live in an age of bitter hatred toward the Bible's teachings. We are bombarded with teachings that contradict the Scripture. Biblical ignorance in the Church is appalling. AND, it appears that the majority have no concern.

So what do we do? Do we ignore the situation? Do we shrug our shoulders and say that we do not agree and then allow the tragic situation to devolve further?

Paul's response to this danger in Thessalonica illustrates what we are to do:

1. Address the issue as soon as you learn about it!

2. Use God's revealed Word to confront the challenges that anarchy presents!

3. Do not ignore its evil or pretend it is a passing fancy!

4. A failure to confront and challenge invites compromise and destruction!

2 Thessalonians urges Christians to encourage, exhort, affirm one another to live loyal devoted and obedient lives in this face of invitations to relent and compromise. This requires (challenges) us to do two things...

1. *Reach out and affirm one another—fellowship!* Fellowship with other saints helps us to maintain a divine perspective.

2. *Be sensitive and perceptive to other brethren—involved!* In 2 Thessalonians 1:4 we find the term "perseverance" which is from the Greek word ὑπομονή and refers to being hopeful; displaying endurance and constancy. This is a compound word and means to "bear up under a heavy load." One is greatly burdened but does not quit> Instead of quitting, he remains steadfast and surefooted.

There is only one secure foundation for mankind struggling through earthly life—"the Rock that is higher than I" (Psalm 61:2). Only by following God can we find the security to trust absolutely in the Truth that the Lord is "faithful" (2 Thessalonians 3:3). When we believe and practice God's authority in our lives, only then can we be absolutely confident in God's sovereignty!

Just as our brethren in Thessalonica, we face false teachings that undermine our confidence. It may not be in regard to the resurrection or end of times theology, but there are those who are doing their best to rethink and redefine and restudy biblical doctrines. And their sole purpose is to remake God in their image! They strive to destroy the foundation of Truth that has provided God's Church with confidence, security, and boldness.

When life threatens discouragement that invites disillusionment and a lessening confidence in God's promises, turn to 2 Thessalonians and reread these three chapters. That will give you hope in the midst of hopelessness! Do not allow Satan's discouraging situations and the Devil's evil associates (the Destructionists; Change Agents; Anarchists) to tempt you to respond "quickly" and surrender your confidence in God. Do not be removed from the security He promises you! "(B)e not quickly shaken from your mind, nor yet be troubled" (2 Thessalonians 2:2)!

Regardless of what goes on in the world, Inspiration urges Christians to follow the actions commanded in 2 Thessalonians 3:13-15...

1. Maintain a strict fellowship

2. Believe a solid doctrinal system

3. Remain active and trusting in God's revealed will and urging others to follow it.

- 12 -

The Destructionist's Heretical Denial

Introduction

The success of modern idolaters hinges upon their ability to redesign, refashion and reword the fundamental doctrines of the Bible. They are motivated by pure selfishness. They demonstrate a rabid disdain for the holy God. They loathe reverence.

But in order to accomplish their diabolical objectives they must destroy the foundations of Truth and provide another system. This process is characterized as "deconstructing the old and reconstructing the new." The problem they face is the Rule of Law governing the current system. So, the first objective in their scheme is to undermine and destroy the governing Rule of Law and then put into place their self-made governing rule of law. In essence they are replacing God with man. This is idolatry pure and simple.

The last lesson discussed how the Destructionists have caused chaos and a "reign of terror" in society, governments, civility, religious institutions and even in the Lord's Church. This devilish destruction is led by those who are governed by anarchy. They respect no laws and honor no boundaries. Here are some traits of those who are seeking to cast aside God's governing Rule of Law:

1. They are "the law" to themselves and each does what is right in his own eyes.

2. They cynically scoff at any Rule of Law that does not support their self-willed desires. They show extreme contempt for any Rule of Law and supporters of that Rule of Law that sets boundaries that they do not like.

Modern Idolaters

3. They terrorize and bully elderships who seek to honor and follow God's Rule of Law.

The focus of the Destructionist is that of a person determined to "deconstruct" the existing framework that sets boundaries for acceptable and unacceptable behavior and beliefs and "reconstruct" the beliefs and organization. The result is that the Almighty God is remade into the image of man,

The anecdotal evidence of the Destructionist upon civil issues is evident in history's darkest pages. The anecdotal evidence of the Destructionist in spiritual issues is tragically repeated throughout civilization's history.

Body

I. Sadly, there have always been those who refused to honor God's spiritual boundaries and conform to God's spiritual commands. Their damnable heresies have constantly split, splintered, and divided the Lord's People. The term "heresy" often connotes the idea of a doctrine that flagrantly violates God's revealed doctrines. But the Greek term from which we get the word "heresy" describes an action that is different from the generally held connotation. This actual meaning is critical to our present discussion.

Titus 3:10 is given this translation: "A man that is an heretic after the first and second admonition reject" (KJV); "A factious man after a first and second admonition refuse" (ASV; NASB).

In Titus 3 Inspiration describes the personality of one who is the "Destructionist" in Crete.

It is interesting that "man" (Titus 3:10) is the term for "mankind" and thus includes both genders. There have been some extremely factious females who thought this did not apply to them because of the translation of "anthropos" by our gender specific "man." The point is clear! Any member of the local congregation can become a factious leader (Hebrews 12:14ff).

The term "factious" is interesting to consider and this is the only reference where it is used in the New Testament. It is from the Greek αἱρετικός (hairetikos) from which we derive our English term "heretic." Hence, the translation in the King James Version as "heretick."

Paul is saying that those who fuel opposition to the governing beliefs and behaviors that are commanded and consistent with the Holy Scriptures are "heretics" in God's Church.

This Greek term refers to an opinionated propagandist who promotes dissension by stubbornness. This term has evolved to refer to one who upholds teachings and expressions contrary to sound doctrine. The evolution of the term is understandable as the process of factionalism is considered. The factious (heretical) person begins voicing opposition and disagreement within the congregation. This voiced disagreement is fueled by anarchy's temptation and fed by pride. It becomes stronger and searches for support from other members. It is relentless in seeking to deconstruct the prevailing pattern of belief and behavior and replace the old system of belief and behavior with anarchy's new idolatry.

Soon the Devil provides the occasion to act on their evil inclinations. Several that share the factious feelings gravitate and soon become associated together. In their criticizing clique the faction's anarchy becomes more entrenched. They feast on negative criticisms and arrogantly decide what is "best" for the congregation. Ultimately battle lines are drawn within the congregation. Eventually the solidarity of the godly eldership is breached and the fellowship is fractured.

Seeking to validate its rebellion to God's structured authority, the factious group begins to justify its criticism of the eldership. The factious group must show that the elders were scripturally wrong or they have to admit they have split the local congregation over foolish questions. Their pride prevents them from admitting they are to blame and so they are compelled to discover "fresh" ideas on old doctrines and begin saying that the elders' prior decisions are unscriptural. They rethink, redesign, and refashion their idolatrous religious ideas.

Soon a doctrinal separation evolves and the factious group begins teaching and preaching a different doctrine (1 Timothy 1:3; 6:3). Consequently, the "different doctrine" has divided the group of God's People into factions and a "heresy" is present.

What began as a simple difference of opinion was manipulated by anarchy's arrogant idolatry and became a damnable doctrine. One whose stubborn, opinionated words are spoken to show how wrong the elders are in their decisions is literally (in the Greek) a "heretic." What a frightful conclusion!

"A heretic is a man of contumacious spirit, self-willed, and contending for his own theories, though they are opposed and contradictory to the universally received doctrines of the Church and the unmistakable revelations of the word of God...We cannot help a man who refuses the kindliest suggestions, and to be controlled by anything but his own wild, ungovernable temper" (Barlow, 103).

The factious person (the heretic) is the member in the congregation who becomes upset with the eldership and in his self-will thinks he is right and the elders are wrong. Then a campaign is commenced by which he goes from person to person in the congregation striving to win support and sympathy. Members are confronted by this person and forced to make a choice: "Will you agree with me that I'm right and the elders are wrong?" (See Galatians 5:20; Hebrews 12:14ff.)

Such a diabolical pattern was foretold as wrecking ruin within local congregations as the governing eldership would compromise God's absolute Rule of Law—"from among your own selves shall men arise, speaking perverse things, to draw away the disciples after them" (Acts 20:30).

Listen to these inescapable conclusions...

- The result of casting aside God's Rule of Law in spiritual belief and behavior is frighteningly summarized by this devilish characterization—it is HERESY!

- All who seek to turn away from God's governing of belief and behavior as taught in the Bible are HERETICS and they face a DAMNABLE destiny!

Establishing this conclusion as an absolute Truth is Inspiration's somber caution: "Whosoever goeth onward and abideth not in the teaching of Christ, hath not God: he that abideth in the teaching, the same hath both the Father and the Son. If anyone cometh unto you, and bringeth not this teaching, receive him not into your house, and give him no greeting: for he that giveth him greeting partaketh in his evil works" (2 John 9-11, ASV).

The basic issue involved is that fellowship IS limited by "the doctrine of Christ." God states that one is not at liberty to pick and choose his religious beliefs, expressions, and fellowship as if he was in a cafeteria's buffet line!

The foundation of this evil spiritual anarchy is found in the Garden's account (see previous lesson). However, Satan has tenaciously persisted throughout mankind's civilization urging man to reject God's Rule of Law and exalt man's wisdom in its place (See 1 Corinthians 2:1-16). Satan's efforts to overthrow God's Rule of Law are evidenced by a casual reading of the Scriptures. Many have been tempted with and succumbed to the devilish cunning to reject and redesign God's commands and then replace God's commands with man's modified beliefs and behaviors.

Anarchy's attack upon the Rule of Law is not isolated to spiritual beliefs and behaviors. It is first evident in culture; then it becomes visible in the Church. When the Rule of Law in a society is ignored, it soon follows that the Rule of Law in the Lord's Church will be ignored.

This is evident in the anarchy that has invaded the Church today. Many today are willing to cast aside the old paths without even considering why they should be followed (Jeremiah 6:16, 17) just as modern culture has cast aside the old rules and boundaries of civil governing

The manner by which the old is cast aside and anarchy is enthroned varies. Some do it with an outright blasphemous rejection saying they "will not follow" what the Bible teaches. They attempt a weak justification of such blasphemy by saying the Bible is antiquated and not applicable to modern society.

Others attempt a path of rejection that is not as obvious in their anarchy. They attempt to offer "insight" and "reinterpretations" of Scripture that will justify their self-willed idolatry. (Peter characterized such as "wresting" the Scriptures 2 Peter 3:16.) Even in Peter's day anarchists were attempting to change the commands of God.

The Greek term Inspiration used (2 Peter 3:16) is στρεβλόω (strebloō) and refers to the form of torture by the rack in which the victim's body was twisted and broken. This term is used to communicate the idea that the spiritual anarchists were not content to accept the simple commands of God, so they "twisted" or "broke" the body of teaching. A suitable term to translate this meaning is they "pervert" or "wrest" the Scriptures to their own ideas.

The twisting of Scripture in recent times is shocking. I cannot think of one doctrine of the New Testament that has not been attacked and perverted by the blasphemous tortuous twisting of the Destructionists/Anarchists/Change Agents.

One of the "new" discoveries of the Destructionists in recent times has been the teaching that there is a difference between what God commanded in the First Century and what He commands now. Or, put in another form such heretics ask "What are the essentials (core teachings) that God requires?" They see some commands as "small stuff" and they claim "God doesn't sweat the small stuff!"

According to the Destructionist, God's Bible has commands and doctrines that apply to the Christian that are non-negotiable and other doctrines and commands are on the periphery and inconsequential. The Destructionists take this point and apply it to efforts to reject binding doctrine and fashion their own Rule of Law.

They deliberately ignore valid biblical commands insisting they have attained the spiritual enlightenment and are able to veto God's commanded essentials and follow only their redesigned commanded essentials (in their own words "the core doctrines" required by God).

The text under consideration in this lesson (2 John 9-11) is the flashpoint for those wishing to go beyond what is written or those wishing to wrest the Scriptures to permit their blasphemous repudiation of loyalty to God's governing Law.

The focus is the simple phrase "the doctrine of Christ." One's response to God's Rule of Law is decided by accepting one of two queries. "Is this the doctrine ABOUT Christ?" (His incarnation). Or, "Is this the doctrine OF Christ?" (His teachings binding upon His followers).

The Destructionists/Anarchist attempts to make the argument that the prohibition in fellowship applies only to those who deny Christ is the incarnate Son of God. They see tests of fellowship limited to a litmus test regarding the Savior's deity. Thus, according to the Progressive Destructionist, if anyone believes that Jesus is the Christ then he must be fellowshipped regardless of other beliefs or behaviors he demonstrates (he bows at the idol of the god of his understanding). According to this position, there are no other boundaries of fellowship. This point is maintained because the Destructionist/Anarchist wishes to change or deny Christ's doctrines in regard to salvation, worship, the exclusiveness of His Church, and life style choices. To the Anarchists, if one believes that Christ is the Son of God then there is no reason fellowship should be restricted. So the Anarchist limits fellowship but his limits are those which allow anything except an outright denial of Christ's humanity (he thus designs God into a more comfortable doctrine).

Thus, fellowship **IS** limited by "the doctrine of Christ." But the perplexity that is presented asks "WHAT IS the doctrine of Christ that limits fellowship?"

This dilemma is not as perplexing as those opposed to the New Testament commands and practices would lead people to believe. The issue is not that confused.

There is only a problem with 2 John 9-11 IF one seeks to justify his anarchy in the local congregation.

Look at the following points and see the clarity of God's Word and the blasphemous confusion and self-contradictions of spiritual anarchy.

Our late brother G. K. Wallace offers an amazing insight into the issue we are examining. In 1963 he delivered a series of lectures at the West End church of Christ in St. Louis, MO. The focus of these lectures was the teaching of W. Carl Ketcherside who was advocating an all-inclusive, none distinctive form of "Christianity" that later led him to establish the "Oak Hill Church" in St. Luis (a community church and not a New Testament Church). Brother Wallace's observations are based upon the unchanging Truth of God's Word and, consequently, are as pertinent today as in 1963! Listen to his observations that have a remarkable bearing on our current discussion.

"Here is the basis of unity as revealed in the New Testament. In Acts 2:42 and 43...The early church based fellowship on continuing in what the apostles taught. They had not only received what the apostles taught, they stayed in it. They continued steadfastly in the apostles' doctrine. The apostles' doctrine included breaking of bread, prayer, the Lord's Supper, and only vocal music. In I Corinthians 14:37 Paul says... They continued in the apostles' doctrine, which included right conduct, right worship, prayer, the breaking of bread.

"Not only that, if they continued in the apostles' doctrine, they had fellowship with each other. John says in I John 1:3...They say fellowship is only with Christ, but John says it is also with us. 'Yea and our...We have a fellowship not only with God, but with one another and with his son, Jesus Christ.' Verse 6...Fellowship according to God, Christ and the Holy Spirit is walking in the light, walking in the truth, and walking after the commandments. Let me read another passage from II John, 'I rejoice'...Jesus said, 'Thy word'...(John 17:17). The truth of God is the word of Christ. New Testament fellowship is built upon walking in the light, walking in the truth, and John says, 'walking in the truth as we received commandment.' It is a fellowship based upon keeping the commandments of Christ, 'And I beseech thee'...Thus, the basis of fellowship is continuing, not just starting in the apostles' doctrine.

"What is the basis of fellowship? It is walking in the light, walking in the truth, and walking after the commandments. Then watch this climax: 'Whosoever goeth onward'…John says whosoever goeth onward and abideth not in the teachings of Christ hath not God.

"Now here in II John 9, is the only serious effort that these brethren make toward the establishment of their theory. They say that the only basis of Christian unity is the acceptance of the deity of Christ. When a man 'goeth onward and abideth not in the teachings of Christ,' they say that means they merely reject the deity of Christ. The real question then is does the phrase 'abideth not in the teachings of Christ' have reference simply to the deity of Christ, or to the doctrine or teachings of the Lord Jesus Christ as revealed in the Bible?" (Wallace, 29).

Wallace's words are indeed a remarkable comment to our current situation!

Alan Highers offered a perceptive comment stating: *"Some simply do not want to believe that Christ's doctrine is binding, especially with regard to some of their practices and ideas. To 'get around' II John 9, they simply limit 'the doctrine of Christ' to what they regard as basic teaching about Christ—that He took on the robe of flesh and came into this world. So long as one believes this basic truth, he 'hath both the Father and the Son.' In this way they can justify, rationalize, and have fellowship with all their denominational friends and colleagues and the pastor down the street who has never been immersed. They want to travel the broad way and choose the easy path instead of doing the hard work of searching the scriptures and abiding in the doctrine of Christ"* (Highers, 47).

The application of this wrested text is being applied not only to the removal of the lines of exclusive fellowship between God's Church and the churches of the world, but it is now being used in a contrived way to applaud, encourage, and permit fellowship with those identified with the churches of Christ who are participating in sins. Using this same tortured interpretation of the Bible, some have arisen echoing the immoral pro-homosexual propaganda saying that if a practicing homosexual comes then he must be received as a saved brother in the Lord IF he believes that Christ was God's incarnate Son! Some congregations even have appointed "couples" as Deacons in the church. This egregious inclusion of the practicing homosexuals is a logical consequence to the twisting of 2 John 9-11 that permits an inclusive fellowship based only on the deity of Christ.

The consequences of redefining "the doctrine of Christ" are far-reaching and will ultimately result in the overthrow of EVERY condition of fellowship and they erase every boundary guarding fellowship that is to maintain "holy living"!

If one is not authorized by God's governing doctrines to judge what is right and what is wrong, then how can one obey Ephesians 5:17?

Upon what basis can one "reprove" and how can we determine what "unrighteousness" is and what distinguishes between "evil" and "good."

Even the demons "believe" that Christ is the Son of God. But we are not to be joined with those who do evil (2 Corinthians 6:14-18). So if belief in the incarnation is the only criterion governing fellowship, then God has placed Christians in an impossible position and that contradiction proves that such a One CANNOT be God!

The revisionary script for "the doctrine of Christ" is thus exposed as an evil addition/subtraction (redesigned idolatry) of God's Holy Truth (Revelation 22:19)!

II. CONSIDER THE GREEK GRAMMAR OF 2 JOHN 9-11

This point is not readily recognized but it resolves the issue. This question involves the consideration of several points of the Greek text.

"The expression 'doctrine of Christ' is the translation of the Greek expression tei didachei tou Christou. Tei didache is the dative case after the preposition en, translated "in." Tou Christou is the genitive case connected with the preceding tei didachei. The nature of this connection is the point at issue. Insomuch as tou Christou is a genitive case, some explanation to the genitive case in general and in this verse must be given.

"Robertson, Grammar, pages 493 states, 'It is the specifying case.' This is the basic idea of the case, but in what way does it specify in II John 9? To understand this, one must notice that the genitive case can be used in connection with a preceding noun; in II John 9 the noun being 'doctrine,' didache. When so connected with a noun or substantive, the genitive case can denote possession, describe, or define" (Wallace, 49-50; citing Robertson, 495-499 sic).

Thus, the term "doctrine of Christ" refers to the doctrine possessed, defined, or specified by Christ.

The genitive case can be in the "objective" or "subjective." In light of the current efforts of the Destructionist's to deconstruct God's Rule of Law and reconstruct his anarchistic rule of Law, these two terms must be understood.

The term "substantive" is defined by Dana and Mantey (78) in these words: *"We have the subjective genitive when the noun in the genitive produces the action, being thus related as object to the verbal idea in the noun modified."*

"The term 'objective' is defined by the same writers on the same page. We have this construction (objective genitive) when the noun in the genitive receives the action, being thus related as object to the verbal idea in the noun modified" (Wallace, 50).

Remember the noun is "doctrine."

So how does this insight from the Greek grammar help us in deciding exactly what "the doctrine of Christ" references in 2 John 9-11? Brother Wallace observes, "In the case of II John 9, the issue thus is: Is the expression 'of Christ' subjective or objective genitive? Thus did Christ produce the action of the noun 'teaching,' subjective; or is he the object of the 'teaching,' objective?

"With this set before you, I wish now to call your attention to the voice of scholarship in regard to this. Mr. Brooke Foss Westcott, co-editor of Westcott and Hort's Greek Testament says; 'in the doctrine of Christ, the doctrine which Christ brought, and which He brought first in His own person, and then through his

followers (Heb. 2:3). This sense seems better than the doctrine of (concerning) the Christ, and the usage of the New Testament is uniformly in favor of it. Revelation 2:14 & 15; John 18:19; Acts 2:42." (Wallace, 50).

Brother Wallace proceeds to give a lengthy list and quotes from renowned Greek scholars and grammarians showing that the "genitive objective" is the only proper interpretation.

The fact that "the doctrine of Christ" is the genitive objective use will be shown later in this article to show incontrovertible proof that John is referencing the "doctrines taught/binding of Christ" upon His Church.

The conclusion from this discussion of the Greek grammar is that this passage (2 John 9-11) teaches that the "doctrine" in view is that doctrine which has Christ as its author and is not teaching concerning the deity of Christ.

To maintain that this verse focuses upon the incarnation of Christ assumes a position that contradicts the best authorities on the meaning of the Greek New Testament. It is a position that arrogates to itself a spiritual anarchy that "twists" or "perverts" the simple teaching of the Scripture.

Those seeking to evade the spiritual Rule of Law, that sets boundaries and restricts fellowship to those who follow the doctrine (beliefs and behaviors) taught by Christ, His Apostles, and the pen of Inspiration, expose their blasphemous attitude and their destructionist agenda by saying the "doctrine OF Christ" does not mean the prescribed beliefs and behaviors commanded in the Bible. They stand in an inexcusable position!

Complementing G. K. Wallace's study is the following observation from brother Guy N. Woods.

"It is the doctrine which Christ personally, and through his disciples, taught—the message of salvation. It is most certainly not the genitive of the object, but of the subject, and signifies the doctrine which Christ originated and propagated through his chosen representatives.

"As the 'doctrine of Balaam' was the doctrine which Balaam taught (Revelation 2:14), so 'the doctrine of Christ' is the doctrine which Christ taught either personally or through agency. This is the uniform usage of the New Testament. See for example, John 18:19; Luke 4:32; Mark 11:18 and Matthew 22:33. These allusions to 'his doctrine,' make clear the significance of the phrase, 'the doctrine of Christ.' Thus, the words, 'doctrine of Christ,' simply mean 'the doctrine which is Christ's'—that body of teaching for which Christ is responsible.

"Only those who want a wider fellowship than the teaching (doctrine) of Christ permits have ever argued otherwise. It is significant that the word 'transgresseth' in this passage derives from a Greek word (proago) whence comes our English word progressive. Thus, literally, 'Whosoever becomes progressive and abides not in the doctrine of Christ has not God.'

"Some rejoice in their progressive stance in religion; but the real choice is between God and errorists. To fellowship those who teach false doctrine is to lose one's fellowship with God.

"Religionists often boast of their progressiveness in religion, and movements in and out of the church has risen based on the concept of progressiveness.

"Progress is proper only when it is in the direction of Christ; and in some matters it is infinitely better to be non-progressive, particularly in not going beyond what the Lord has said.

"John makes clear that any movement which is away from the teaching of Christ is progress in the wrong direction, and results in the loss of God himself. We must ever be on guard against any semblance of departure from 'the doctrine of Christ'—his teaching as set out in the New Testament" (Woods, 267-268).

It is significant that Inspiration chose one unique term to identify those who blasphemously cast aside God's commanded belief and behaviors—the word chosen is "progressive" (παραβαίνω—parabaino).

How disturbing the thought is that those who are pushing the Destructionist/Anarchist agenda today take great pride in becoming "progressive." They boast in the very word that is used by Inspiration to communicate damnation! Is this single fact not enough to convict those seeking to deconstruct the old paths and reconstruct the new progressive changes in the local congregations?

Brother Dave Miller observes, *"Another passage sometimes used to foster fellowship with the denominations is verse nine of Second John. The expression 'doctrine of Christ:' has typically been taken to mean the entirety of Christian doctrine (known in Greek as the subjective genitive). Consequently, fellowship is not to be extended to those who deviate on any point of Christ's doctrine. Those promoting change in the church insist, however, that 'doctrine of Christ' refers specifically and exclusively to the single doctrine* **about** *Christ (objective genitive) that some were denying, namely, that Christ had come in the flesh. They reason that the only basis upon which fellowship between Christians may be disrupted is when an individual denies the incarnation or person of Jesus. They say fellowship should not be breached on other matters such as the use of instrumental music in worship, women preachers, etc.*

"The overwhelming verdict of scholarship is that the phrase 'doctrine of Christ' in the ninth verse of Second John refers to the **whole** *of Christian doctrine"* (Miller, 301).

"Regardless of what other men say, what evidence exists within the Bible itself to assist in understanding the meaning of the expression 'doctrine of Christ'? The term didache is used thirty times in the New Testament. The most common subjective genitive form is 'the doctrine of him,' i.e. 'his doctrine' (cf. 'my doctrine' and 'your doctrine'). The 'doctrine of Christ' also parallels 'the doctrine of the apostles' (Acts 2:42) and 'the doctrine of the Lord' (Acts 13:12). The same subjective genitive is seen in the expressions 'the doctrine of the Pharisees and Scribes' (Matt. 16:12), 'the doctrine of Balaam' (Rev. 2:14) and 'the doctrine of the Nicolaitans' (Rev. 2:15). These latter two are further instances of the use of the subjective genitive specifically in John's writings. All of these examples parallel the

expression 'doctrine of Christ' and refer to the totality of teaching--what the person taught" (Miller, 303-304).

"As suggested in some of the foregoing comments, the construction of objective genitive (the doctrine about Christ rather than the doctrine which Christ taught) seems to be contrived to fit the theology of the proponent rather than to fit the context of John's epistles" (Highers, 47).

III. CONSIDER THE CONTEXT OF 2 JOHN 9-11

Christian fellowship is the most powerful force in Christianity. It maintains boldness and assurance. It encourages and edifies. It portends the environment of Heaven's splendor. It encourages steadfast loyalty, devotion, and obedience to God's Rule of Law.

The fellowship that binds the Lord's Church together in strength, unity, and loyalty can also be a factor that brings destruction to the congregation if that fellowship is not guarded. The Church cannot fellowship those who are false teachers because they bring into the congregation beliefs and behaviors that compromise and weaken the congregation's strength. These become as leaven and lead to the destruction of the faith that others have. False teaching has historically been shown to produce actions by which people move away from God. The false teachers stir up parties and factions that lead to divisions (hence they are heretics).

The failure to maintain loyalty to God's doctrine has historically proven destructive. Thus the warning: "Thou shalt not follow a multitude to do evil; neither shalt thou speak in a cause to turn aside after a multitude to wrest justice" (Exodus 23:2, ASV). And again: "Take heed unto yourselves, and to all the flock, in which the Holy Spirit hath made you bishops, to feed the church of the Lord which he purchased with his own blood. I know that after my departing grievous wolves shall enter in among you, not sparing the flock; and from among your own selves shall men arise, speaking perverse things, to draw away the disciples after them" (Acts 20:28-30, ASV).

The Epistles of John were written to guard the bond of fellowship that God has designed for His Church. There are several repeated expressions in these Epistles. Perhaps the term that is focused upon more than others in John's Epistles is the word "love." For this reason many commentaries on these Epistles includes the word "love."

The sacred fellowship guarding the Lord's Church is indeed governed by "love." John's First Epistle stresses the fact that the brotherhood of believers is demonstrated by love of one to another. John's Second and Third Epistles stress the fact that the fellowship of believers is guarded by a love of the Truth.

A critical contextual fact in John's Epistles is that fellowship must be maintained by the love that brethren show to one another AND by the love that brethren show in obeying the Truth of God. It is NOT a sign of Christian love to tolerate either acts of bitterness, ignorance of brethren's needs, or false teachers. These are shown by John to be elements of evil that corrupt God's Church.

In fact, it is a sign of a LACK (or absence) of love to permit or turn a blind eye to the teachers seeking to bring in damnable doctrines. Using Truth to refute the false teacher is not the act of a hateful person but the conduct of a loving friend.

Brother Jimmy Jividen accurately observes, *"Condoning false teachers in the church is not a sign of tolerance and love. It is a sign of the compromising fear of men and a blatant disrespect for the authority of Christ"* (Jividen, 98)

The immediate context of John's Epistles can be summarized as Inspiration's warning against three devilish temptations that will destroy God's Church:

- First John—Avoid false love

- Second John—Avoid false teachers

- Third John—Avoid false gospels (messages)

A good summary of the contextual elements of 2 John 9-11 is offered in this analysis: "The theme of John's second letter is false love and false doctrine. In the first letter John has shown that the love of the brethren was a vital principle of Christianity. In the second letter, he explains that true love does not condone nor encourage false doctrine. Love must be in truth. Christians are bound to one another by the special bond of truth. Truth is the basis of Christian love. John stresses this by the fact that he mentions the word "truth" four times in the first three verses. Christians do not love each other because they are drawn together by fleshly ties or social standing, but because of the truth they have in common. Christians are bound together in love because objective truth teaches it. Truth is a spiritual force which abides within (verse 2). It is a continuing principle which directs because it will remain forever. Love as an abiding principle remains among brethren as long as truth endures; thus Christian love is founded upon the truth" (Camp, 233).

In the history of the Lord's Church many have chosen to think they were not bound by the "doctrines" of the New Testament (those commanded by Christ, communicated by the Apostles, and inscribed by pens of Inspiration).

The prominent false doctrine that John addressed was Gnosticism. This philosophy denied the basic elements of New Testament Christianity. It stressed that the fleshly environment was inconsequential to one's spiritual relationship with God. In fact it was repulsed that any material (earthly/worldly) factors had any bearing to one's spirituality. Thus, they would tolerate any worldly behavior saying that the fleshly has nothing to do with the spiritual; it was a philosophy that granted freedom for fleshly indulgences. Such fittingly illustrates anarchy (modern idolatry) in its clearest demonstration. So determined were the Gnostics to follow this evil that they denied that our Lord came in a fleshly body.

The Gnostic heresy (factious dividing by unscriptural belief and practice) was compromising the brethren to whom John wrote his general epistles. John's Epistles challenge this error and silence its advocacy.

In his First Epistle John points out the error of Gnostic beliefs showing that Christ was indeed on earth in a fleshly body that could be touched. The First Epistle continues to show that one must be involved in the earthly affairs of others because that is what true love does. You simply cannot divorce the earthly from the spiritual. What you do on earth impacts the spiritual. You cannot say you love God and fail to demonstrate this love on earth.

First, John stresses this fact--Anarchy does not allow you to hate you brother. Earthly relationships have an absolute impact upon the spiritual relationships.

In his Second Epistle John points out that "love" cannot be permitted to condone compromise in behaviors and beliefs. In order for earthly behavior to compliment spiritual beliefs and behaviors, one must obey the prescribed commands (doctrines). If one refuses to follow the prescribed commands (doctrine), that prevents the spiritual relationship.

Second, John stresses this fact--Anarchy does not allow you to pick and choose which doctrines you will follow. Earthly beliefs and behaviors have an absolute impact upon the spiritual relationships.

In his Third Epistle John points out that no matter how alluring other gospels may seem, they must not be permitted. The one true Message of God has been "once for all delivered" and stands as the foundation of earthly and spiritual belief and behaviors!

Third, John stresses the fact--Anarchy does not permit you to treat the Inspired Word of God with callous indifference and follow another Rule of Law. Earthly governing of spiritual beliefs and behaviors has an absolute Rule of Law that has an absolute impact upon spiritual relationships.

Those who hold to the position that the "doctrine of Christ" in 2 John 9-11 applies ONLY to the incarnation of Christ miss the point that while John did address the Gnostic heresy that was not the only error he addressed. *"John dealt with the error of those who claimed they had no sin (I Jn. 1:8-10), he rebuked those who said they could know Christ without obeying his commandments (I Jn. 2:4), he condemned those who hated their brethren while pretending to walk in the light (I Jn. 2:9-11). In other words, the denial that Jesus came in the flesh is not the only false doctrine that John contrasted with the doctrine of Christ. It is fiction to assert that John was only warning and admonishing about whether Jesus came in the flesh"* (Highers, 46).

Brother Highers continues saying, "Further, take a look at other expressions John uses in his second epistle along with his reference to 'the doctrine of Christ.' He speaks of 'the truth,' 'have known the truth,' 'the truth's sake,' 'in truth and love,' and 'walking in truth' (II Jn. 1-4). He refers to 'a commandment from the Father,' 'walk after his commandments,' 'this is the commandment' (II Jn. 4-6). Consider these together:

(1) John speaks of 'the truth' (verses 1-4).

(2) He speaks of 'the commandments' (verses 4-6).

(3) He follows, then, with a reference to 'the doctrine of Christ'(verses 9-10).

"If one has regard for the contextual surroundings of the passage under consideration, he would have to recognize the connection between 'the truth,' 'the commandments,' and 'the doctrine of Christ.' It is clear that the terms are used together in such a brief epistle to denote the same idea—namely, the body of truth taught and revealed by the Lord.

"These expressions certainly include more than the fact of Jesus coming in the flesh. The whole context of II John 9 weighs heavily against the conclusion that John intends to refer not only to 'the doctrine of Christ,' but to 'the doctrine, truth, and commandments' which Jesus taught" (Highers, 46).

Brother Jimmy Jividen accurately observes this truth regarding the consequences of limiting the immediate context of 2 John 9-11 only to the incarnation of Christ. "If John were teaching that the only criterion for fellowship is confessing that Jesus came in the flesh, some serious theological problems would follow.

"If such an understanding is correct, then one must have fellowship with demons. They are believers in Jesus Christ (1 Corinthians 3:16, 17).

"If such an understanding is correct, then one has fellowship with those whom Jesus does not know. The non-doers of God's will are not recognized by Jesus as being His disciples (Ephesians 5:27).

"If such an understanding is correct, then one must have fellowship with those God does not know. Those who claim to know Him but refuse to keep His commandments are liars. No matter how emotional their claim, refusal to keep His commandments and His word alienates one from God (Matthew 21:12, 13).

"Condoning false teachers in the church is not a sign of tolerance and love. It is a sign of the compromising fear of men and a blatant disrespect for the authority of Christ" (Jividen, 98)

The immediate context clearly shows that "the doctrine of Christ" refers to the totality of the teachings, commands, and doctrine which originated with the Lord's teachings and was transmitted to the Apostles by the Holy Spirit and to the world through Inspiration's writings in the Bible.

"The word 'doctrine' is used twice in II John 9, 10: First, 'whosoever abideth not in the doctrine of Christ hath not God.' And second, 'whosoever abideth in the doctrine of Christ hath both the Father and the Son." Whatever 'the doctrine of Christ" means in the first part of the passage, it means in the latter. If the first allusion to 'the doctrine of Christ" refers only to his coming in the flesh, and one who abides not in this doctrine 'hath not God,' then all that one in the latter part of the passage must do to have both the Father and the Son is to abide in the doctrine that Christ came in the flesh. This would amount to salvation by faith only" (Highers, 47).

The remote context offers strong support for the conclusions derived from the immediate context. The tragedy that John 9-11 addresses is that teachers/leaders had come into the congregation with a "different" belief and behavior doctrine. John labels them as "deceivers" (verse 7) because they sought to present their "new" doctrines as the doctrine delivered by Christ. These had become "progressive" in their efforts to redefine and rethink the doctrine of Christ which commands specific beliefs and behaviors. The urgency of confronting these "progressives" is stated in blunt terms. They are going to harm the Church so brethren have the obligation to preempt the intrusion and refuse the redefined doctrines. This compliments the account of the gold calf idolatry—Moses told Aaron that such idolatrous actions should have been confronted and never allowed to happen.

How does the remote context of Scriptures confirm this principle of confronting false teaching?

God expects His People to judge the teachers and doctrines and test them (Matthew 7:15-20; 1 John 4:1). Upon what Rule of Law are these to be tested? The Rule of Law that decides these matters is the "doctrine of Christ." If one interprets this as meaning only belief in the incarnation of Christ then we are without any criterion to judge/test any other spiritual belief or behavior! How would one say any behavior is wrong as long as the one coming professes to accept the incarnation of Christ?

God expects His People to confront and expose beliefs and behavior that are contrary to His commands (Ephesians 5:3-11). But by what Rule of Law are we to do this if "the doctrine of Christ" does not refer to His commands, teachings and doctrines of belief and behavior?

God expects His People to be able to discern when the Scriptures are "wrested" and avoid the false teaching (2 Peter 3:16; Romans 16:18; 1 Timothy 1:20; 5:20; 2 Timothy 4:10). But how can Christians "discern" what is false if the only standard is one's belief in the incarnation of Christ.

God expects His People to renounce and abstain from all works of evil and flesh (Galatians 6:16-21; 1 Corinthians 3:9-11; 2 Corinthians 6:14-18; Romans 1:29-32). But upon what authority can Christians do this if they do not have an absolute Rule of Law? According to the Progressives, anyone coming into a congregation must be welcomed and involved as a partner as long as that one believes in the incarnation. This invites the congregation to be populated by all manner of sin and immorality!

God expects His People to "abide in Christ's Word" (John 8:31, 32). But how can Christians do this if there is only one absolute criterion and that only addresses His incarnation and not the words, teachings, commands, and truth that He taught?

God expects His People to not to become "partakers of other men's sins" (1 Timothy 5:22). But how is this possible if the only "sin" is the denial of Christ's incarnation?

Once again brother Franklin Camp has insight that offers clarity to the remote context this passage. *"The Bible is its own commentary. The New Testament explains the meaning of doctrine. Notice a few passages, 'And it came to pass, when Jesus had ended these sayings, the people were astonished at his doctrine' (Matthew 7:28).*

"The sayings of Jesus are called doctrine. What were the sayings of Jesus referred to? The reference is the entire sermon in chapters 5, 6 and 7. This whole sermon is called doctrine. Is the sermon limited to the teaching about Christ? The sermon contains the teaching of Christ. Here are a few things contained in the sermon, 'The Beatitudes, adultery, divorce, love, prayer, heavenly treasures, earthly treasures, anxiety, false teaching, doing the will of God, hearing and doing.'

"All of these subjects and others are included in the sermon and are called doctrine. Whose doctrine was it? Christ was the preacher; therefore it must follow that the sermon contains the doctrine of Christ. The ones that insist that the doctrine of Christ means only doctrine about Christ must reject the Sermon on the Mount since it's called doctrine and as Christ was the Teacher, it is the doctrine of Christ.

"Christ warned his disciples of the doctrine of the Pharisees and Sadducees. Was he trying to convince his disciples of the being of the Pharisees and Sadducees? Or was he warning of their teaching?

"In I Timothy 4:1 Paul speaks of the doctrine of devils. Is Paul discussing the doctrine about devils or is he speaking of the doctrine that had its origin with devils? Two of the doctrines are mentioned in verse 3.

"The doctrine of Balaam is mentioned in Revelation 2:14. There cannot be any question as to the meaning of the doctrine of Balaam. 'But I have a few things against thee, because thou hast there some that hold the teaching of Balaam, who taught Balak to cast a stumbling block before the children of Israel, to eat things sacrificed to idols, and to commit fornication.'

"The doctrine of Balaam was what Balaam taught. These are only a few of the passages in the New Testament that interpret the meaning of the phrase the doctrine of. The doctrine of Christ was the teaching of Christ (Matthew 7:28). The doctrine of devils was not doctrine about devils, but their teaching. The doctrine of Balaam was not doctrine about Balaam, but what he taught.

"In the light of these passages, what is the doctrine of Christ in II John 9-11? It is the teaching of Christ and the teaching of Christ through the apostles.

"Fellowship involves doctrine and it cannot be limited to the doctrine about Christ.

"These verses demand that false teachers be excluded from fellowship. To fail to do so is to partake of their evil deeds. The attempt that is made by some to limit fellowship to the gospel while making a distinction between gospel and doctrine is denied by II John 9-11. It is high time, instead of listening to these teachers, that we follow the inspired directions given by the apostle John—to refuse fellowship to those that teach false doctrine" (Camp, 234).

IV. PRACTICAL CONSIDERATIONS—QUESTIONS IMPACTING THE CHURCH'S FELLOWSHIP BOUNDARIES

The true test of biblical doctrine is its practicality. The way to expose error is to observe its impracticality. Truth will enhance and govern life in practical life. Error leads to inconsistency and conflict.

As we examine "the doctrine of Christ" under the scope of practicality, its truth and application becomes very clear. The practical application of "the doctrine of Christ" clearly distinguishes which of the interpretations is truth.

First, a matter of practical clarity. Is the deity/incarnation of Christ the ONLY criterion for fellowship/salvation? If the incarnation is the only criterion for fellowship, what about other texts limiting fellowship by other criteria of belief/behavior? By interpreting 2 John 9-11 as referring only to the incarnation of Christ the entire ethical and moral center of Christianity is thrown into chaos. Let the erudite "progressive" tell us WHERE does Christian fellowship begin and end? If one's belief in the incarnation of Christ is the only standard for fellowship, we are permitted to fellowship any mortal or spiritual being who believes that Jesus came in the flesh. But if the "doctrine of Christ" refers to the Lord's teachings, commands, and words communicated by Inspiration, then we can fellowship ONLY those who have not "gone beyond" the written doctrine of the Bible. One must follow Ephesians 5:3-11. So exactly HOW are we to do this? What is the Rule of Law. Is it our own idolatrous rules or is it the written Word of God? The practical and consistent answer is that the doctrine of Christ includes His words, commands and truth that were given to the Apostles and committed to writing in the Bible.

Second, a matter of practical revelation. Those who want to restrict the binding commands only to the "red-letters" of the Gospel or to the deity of Christ, admit they do not have the TOTALITY OF Christ's teachings because Christ Himself admitted that the FULL revelation of His teaching would occur only when the Holy Spirit came and guided the written messages of the New Testament (John 14:26)! Why will one find comfort in an incomplete revelation? Such a position is absurdity gone to seed!

Third, a matter of practical Christian living. Christianity is a lifestyle devoted to holy living. If there is no doctrine to follow except the incarnation of Christ, then Christians are left without a practical guide for holy living. There are certain lifestyles that neither God nor His children can fellowship. How can we decide between the godly and ungodly if the "doctrine of Christ" only applies to His incarnation?

Fourth, it is a matter of practical salvation. As already noted, this observation by brother Highers is most insightful to the practical application of the Anarchists/Destructionists revision of 2 John 9-11. *"The word 'doctrine' is used twice in II John 9, 10: First, 'whosoever abideth not in the doctrine of Christ hath not God.' And second. 'whosoever abideth in the doctrine of Christ hath both the Father and the Son." Whatever 'the doctrine of Christ" means in the first part of the passage, it means in the latter. If the first allusion to 'the doctrine of Christ" refers only to his coming in the flesh, and one who abides not in this doctrine 'hath not God,' then all that one in the latter part of the passage must do to have both the Father and the Son is to abide in the doctrine that Christ came in the flesh. This would amount to salvation by faith only"* (Highers, 47). Hence the modern idolater's ONLY condition for salvation is that one must believe in the incarnation of Christ! Thus, he extends an open and inclusive fellowship to the godless demons!

Fifth, it is a matter of practical fellowship. What will determine fellowship? If the "doctrine of Christ" is only the teaching about His incarnation then that is the only fellowship requirement. The Christian would be compelled to accept and applaud those in the most heinous behaviors if they believed Christ came in the flesh. But such an inclusive fellowship is contradictory to the Bible's requirements of holy living and holy associations. If one does not agree that the "doctrine of Christ" refers to His words, commands, and truth that were given to the Apostles and committed to writing in the Bible, then he has to accept and applaud any belief and behavior as long as one believes that Christ came in the flesh. This point exposes the error of interpreting 2 John 9-11 in the liberal/progressive manner. Maintaining the progressive's interpretation of 2 John 9-11 means fellowship MUST exist in spite of gross sin and immorality...as long as one believes that Christ came in the flesh then he must be fellowshipped and considered a partner in the Gospel!

Can one honestly say that the ONLY basis for fellowship is belief in His incarnation? If so, how does that explain the myriad of other texts commanding that fellowship must be terminated because one is not obeying the "doctrine of Christ"?

Christian fellowship is restricted by MUCH more than simply believing in the incarnation of Christ.

1. Fellowship does not extend to anyone outside of the Body of Christ (Ephesians 2:12; 2 Corinthians 6:17).

2. Fellowship does not extend to a disorderly brother (2 Thessalonians 3:6; 1 Corinthians 5:11-13).

3. Fellowship does not extend to the factious (Titus 3:10, 11). Strife and division are serious offenses and we must refuse fellowship to those who persist in such conduct.

4. Fellowship is not to be extended to false teachers who seek to infiltrate the congregation (Romans 16:17—"to mark" is to fix one's eyes upon; to direct attention to; "to avoid" is to stay away from and have no association or partnership with them). This is exactly what 2 John 9-11 commands.

5. Fellowship is not to embrace false religions (Ephesians 5:11, 12). Denominations fall into this classification—they are a different religion than that found in the New Testament because they honor man's creeds more than the Word of God (See 2 Corinthians 6:14-16).

6. Fellowship does not embrace false worship (Matthew 15:9; 1 Corinthians 10:21; Colossians 2:23).

Sixth, it is a matter of practical obedience to God's commands. It is impossible to obey God's requirements if one interprets 2 John 9-11 as stating the basis for fellowship is only the incarnation of Christ. How can you "rebuke" evil and have no fellowship with the "works" of darkness" when your Rule of Law says such are to be included in the fellowship conditions? How do you remain bold and not timid in standing for the Truth (2 Timothy 1:7) when your Rule of Law condones any belief and every behavior as long as it does not deny the incarnation of Jesus Christ?

Seventh, it is a matter of religious unity. The only way for there to be religious unity is for all concerned to follow exactly what God's Book commands. This was the solution to religious division in the first century. The Corinthian congregation was torn apart by anarchists who followed their own desires. Thus, the warning of Inspiration simply states, "Now these things, brethren, I have in a figure transferred to myself and Apollos for your sakes; that in us ye might learn not to go beyond the things which are written; that no one of you be puffed up for the one against the other" (1 Corinthians 4:6, ASV). The evil anarchy had prompted some to "go beyond the things written." Once again the "progressives" lead away from salvation and into damnation.

The solution to Corinth's religious division was not offering a unity and fellowship on some wrested platform. Unity was to be found ONLY by following the Inspired counsel to the Corinthian congregation, "Now I beseech you, brethren, through the name of our Lord Jesus Christ, that ye all speak the same thing, and that there be no divisions among you; but that ye be perfected together in the same mind and in the same judgment" (1 Corinthians 1:10, ASV).

God NEVER counsels a religious unity with each party holding to different beliefs and behaviors. The only way unity is possible is if all follow the same directions found in "the doctrine of Christ." Only those following these directions will contribute to unity. Those unwilling to follow these directions and who "go beyond" these directions have no part in our fellowship.

"There cannot be an increase of love between brethren by rejecting the truth of the gospel which must be held in common. The present unity movement ignores this vital fact and seeks unity by compromising the truth on which true love and unity depend. It is said that love is blind. The marriage that is entered into in a blind love soon opens the eyes to the tragic consequence of this kind of love. Jesus said, 'If the

blind leads the blind, they both will fall into the ditch' (Matthew 15:14). What is true of blind love in marriage is likewise true in Christianity. Allowing the 'blind lovers' of today to lead will carry the church into the ditch of compromise and apostasy" (Camp, 235)

Conclusion

I. The "doctrine of Christ" is the teachings of the Lord Jesus Christ. These teachings He first spoke and then sent the Holy Spirit to cause the Apostles to remember all He had taught so they could teach it to others. It was this teaching that inspired authors of Holy Scripture were superintended to transcribe in written form so that following generations would have that "doctrine" available for their study and governing.

II. Notice these texts that bring the honest heart to an undeniable conclusion:

A. Matthew 7:28, 29—the people were astonished at His "doctrine" that He had communicated in His "teaching" (nothing in referenced to His incarnation!).

B. Matthew 22:33—they were astonished at His "doctrine" that He had communicated in His "teaching" (nothing in referenced to His incarnation!).

C. Mark 4:2—Christ "taught" His "doctrine" in parables (nothing in referenced to His incarnation!).

D. Mark 11:18—the people were astonished at His "doctrine" which He had communicated in His teachings (nothing in referenced to His incarnation!).

E. Mark 12:38—Christ's "doctrine" involved Him warning about false teachers (nothing in referenced to His incarnation!).

It is an undeniable conclusion that the "doctrine of Christ" involves His teaching commands and truth by the words He spoke! Interpreting "the doctrine of Christ" in 2 John 9-11 in any other way is to cast aside God's Rule of Law and becoming a Destructionist that is controlled by an idolatrous anarchy.

III.   The conclusion of this study is aptly summarized in this observation, *"When one refuses to speak the things which befit sound doctrine (Titus 2:1), and persists in the perverse disputing of men of corrupt minds, and destitute of the truth (1 Timothy 6:5), then we become partakers of his evil deeds (2 John 11) if we refuse to mark and avoid them."* (Powell, 240)

"Even if 'doctrine of Christ' did not refer to all of Christ's teaching in the ninth verse of Second John, the change agents would still have no basis for restricting fellowship to one or a few 'essentials.' Too many other passages teach the same thing in contexts that clearly pertain to doctrines far beyond simply the person/deity of Christ...One example out of many would be First Corinthians chapter five where Paul insists that fellowship between Christians must be disrupted over such matters as fornication, covetousness, extortion, and drunkenness (I Corinthians 5:10-11). None of these items have to do with the person of Christ. Yet the y are clearly treated in Scriptures as matters of fellowship that affect unity" (Miller, 304).

"Paul prayed that the love of the Philippians would abound in knowledge and judgment being able to discriminate between things that differ (Philippians 1:9, 10). This is the same command that John advocates. It is truth that enables one's love to discriminate. Love is not to be so blind as to ignore doctrinal error and the unscriptural conduct of others. John saw no problem of inconsistency in the command to love and refusing fellowship with false teachers. Love is not to destroy loyalty to truth. Love demands loyalty to truth which means love is opposed to error. Christian fellowship includes both love and truth. Neither one is to be sacrificed at the expense of the other. Love grows soft if it is not molded by truth and truth becomes harsh when it is not controlled by love. The scriptural formula, as stated in II John, is to love in truth and to hold the truth in love. It is false love that runs around with error and encourages it" (Camp, 235).

"The doctrine of Christ is the doctrine given him of the Father. For I have not spoken of myself, but the Father which sent me, he gave me a commandment, what

I should say and what I should speak (Jn. 12:49-50). To accept the doctrine of Christ is to receive the teaching of the Father, and to reject the doctrine of Christ is tantamount to rejecting the word of God. Thus, whosoever transgresseth, and abideth not in the doctrine of Christ, hath not God (II Jn. 9)" (Highers, 47).

IV.   As we complete this lesson, we reach a conclusion that is consistent with application of Scriptural' principles in the Old Testament and the New Testament. It is consistent with the exhortation for Christians to live a life of holy devotion because they are separated from the world; and that is consistent with the Almighty God's commands for Christians to be shining lights in a dark world and utilize their light to expose the evil darkness. The consistent conclusion is that "the doctrine of Christ" refers to the totality of the Lord's teachings, commands, and doctrines. These were verbally taught to the Apostles and then further instructed by the Holy Spirit and ultimately committed to the infallible written Word by Inspiration.

It is not the "doctrine ABOUT Christ but the doctrine FROM Christ!

V.   Only by adhering to "the doctrine of Christ" is one able to be saved and live righteously. This truth simply states that only by obeying the totality of God's commands can one be saved and sanctified!

VI.   As was stated centuries ago, but still applicable today, "This is the end of the matter: all hath been heard: fear God, and keep his commandments; for this is the whole duty of man. For God will bring every work into judgment, with every hidden thing, whether it be good, or whether it be evil" (Ecclesiastes 12:13, 14, ASV).

Sources Cited

Barlow, George. *The Preacher's Complete Homiletic Commentary: I-II Timothy, Titus, Philemon.* Grand Rapids, MI: Baker Book House, 1978.

Bellah, Robert N, Richard Madsen and William M. Sullivan. *Habits of the Heart: Individualism and Commitment in American Life,* University of California Press, 1985.

Brown, Frances, Editor with Samuel Rolles Driver and Charles Augustus Briggs, *The New Brown-Drier-Briggs-Gesenius Hebrew-English Lexicon, With an appendix containing the biblical Aramaic.* Peabody, MA: Hendrickson Publishers, 1979.

Calvin, John. *Institutes of the Christian Religion, Book One, trans. Henry Beveridge, USA: Hendrickson, revised edition, 2008.*

Camp, Franklin. "The Letters of John in the Light of Today's Needs," *Freed-Hardeman College 1975 Lectures.* Henderson, TN: Freed-Hardeman College, 1975.

Dana, H.E. and Julius R. Mantey. A Manual Grammar of the Greek New Testament. New York: The Macmillan Company, 1967.

Dillard, Annie. *Teaching Stones to Talk.* New York: Harper & Row, Publishers, 1988.

Excell, Joseph, editor. *The Preacher's Homiletic Commentary.* New York: Funk & Wagnalls Company, 1978.

Foster, Rev. Elon. *New Cyclopaedia of Prose Illustrations.* New York & London: Funk & Wagnalls Company, 1877.

Groeschel, Craig. "#Struggles: Following Jesus in a Selfie-Centered World." *Devotionals Daily* (February 6, 2016). HarperCollins Christian Publishing, 501 Nelson Place, Nashville, TN, 37214. Accessed online February 6, 2016.

Harris, R. Laird, Editor. *Theological Wordbook of the Old Testament,* Chicago: Moody Press, Volume 1, 1980.

Highers, Alan. *The Spiritual Sword.* "From the Woodlands." Memphis, TN: Getwell Church of Christ, 2012.

Houston Chronicle, November 3, 1988, Special Five-Part Series, "Willie: An Autobiography."

Houston Chronicle, June 27, 1998, Mini Page.

Jividen, Jimmy. *Koinonia: A Place of Tough and Tender Love*. Nashville, TN: Gospel Advocate Company, 1989.

Keegan, John. *The First World War*. New York: Alford A. Knopf, 1999.

Lomis, Stanley. *Paris in the Terror: June 1793-July 1794*. J.B. Lippincott Company, Philadelphia & New York, 1964.

McFague, Sallie. *Models of God—Theology for an Ecological, Nuclear Age*. Minneapolis, MN: Augsburg Fortress Publishing, 1987.

Miller, Dave. *Piloting the Strait: A Guidebook for Assessing Change in Churches of Christ*. Pulaski, TN: Sain Publications, 1996.

O'Rourke, P.J. *Parliament of Whores*. Boston: Atlantic Monthly Press, 1991.

Page, Dr. Frank S. *"Taking the Moral Pulse."* Nashville, TN: *Leadership* SBC Life (A Journal of the Southern Baptist Conference), May 1999.

Powell, Ivie. "Unity in Diversity Error." *1999 Memphis School of Preaching Lectureship*. Pulaski, TN: Sain Publications, 1999.

Robertson, A.T. *Grammar of the Greek New Testament in the Light of Historical Research, Third Edition*. London: Hodder & Stoughton, MCMXIX.

Smith, F. LaGuard. *The Cultural Church*. Nashville, TN: Nashville, TN: 20th Century Christian, 1992.

Vine, W.E. *Isaiah: Prophecies, Promises, Warnings*. Grand Rapids, MI: Lamplighter Books, Zondervan Publishing House, reprint 1971.

Wallace, G.K. *A Critical Review of a New (Old) Modernism and a Plea for Unity*. St. Louis, MO: West End church of Christ, 1963.

Woods, Guy N. *Questions & Answers, Volume II*. Nashville, TN: Gospel Advocate Co., 1986.

Wuthnow, Robert. *"Small Groups Forge Notions...of the Sacred,"* Christian Century, December 8, 1993, Volume 110, No. 35, 1239-1240.

About the Author

John L. Kachelman, Jr. has worked with congregations in Alabama, Arkansas, Missouri, Kentucky and Tennessee and he continues to speak regularly at various congregations, lectureships and gospel meetings. He is a graduate ('76) of Freed-Hardeman University and has written many books, lesson series, and articles for religious publications.

Since 1994, John has worked closely with evangelism in Ukraine. His many trips have helped establish congregations and provide continued teaching for spiritual growth. He has also helped coordinate efforts to provide humanitarian aid distributed through local congregations in Ukraine and other countries around the world. As a point-man in helping coordinate these humanitarian shipments to other countries, he works to collect donated items and ship them to faithful congregations in the receiving countries. He works to insure that all benevolent aid is distributed by local Christians and the Lord's Church receives credit for the good accomplished.

John is married to the former Jennifer Davenport and has four children Brian, John III, Rachel and Rebekah. Check out the Kachelman family website (www.kachelman.com) for more information on his family.

Made in the USA
Middletown, DE
13 January 2020